THE KEY, THE DOOR, AND THE GARDEN

Helping you find your way back to God
and grow in holiness

ANTHONY M. HADEED

THE KEY, THE DOOR, AND THE GARDEN
Copyright © 2022 by Anthony M. Hadeed

All rights reserved, including the right to reproduce this book or portions thereof in any form. A reviewer or author may quote brief passages when writing a review or a book. For further information, contact the publisher via email at info@yourlifepurpose.com.

All Bible references are taken from the Revised Standard Version, Second Catholic Edition (Ignatius Press, 2001).

Hadeed, Anthony M.
   The Key, The Door, and The Garden
   / by Anthony M. Hadeed, M.Sc.

ISBN 978-0-578-83309-5

Subjects: RELIGION / Faith | RELIGION / Christian Living / Personal Growth | RELIGION / Christian Living / Prayer

YourLifePurpose Publishing Centre

Printed in the United States of America

The Key, The Door, and The Garden

"An easy-to-read book written in a conversational style. The author shares his personal experience of six years on the wide road of unbelief while immersed in the world of science that eventually led to the narrow path of belief and fidelity. He gives a powerful guide to all, but especially to those who need help with structure for achieving their dreams, desires, and decisions to draw closer to God in a life-long, loving relationship."

Bishop Malcolm Galt
Emeritus of Bridgetown, Barbados
4 December 2020

"Priests are the officers. You are the soldiers. The hardest fighting is often done by the soldiers, and in wartime against error and sin, the soldier is not always near the officer, and he must be ready to strike without waiting for command. Laymen are not anointed in confirmation to the end that they merely save their own souls and pay their pew rent. They must think, work, organize, read, speak, act, as circumstances demand."

Archbishop John Ireland
St. Paul, Minnesota
A special and emphatic appeal to the laity in a sermon delivered to commemorate the centenary of the American Catholic hierarchy
10 November 1889

"God is opening before the Church the horizons of a humanity more fully prepared for the sowing of the Gospel. I sense that the moment has come to commit all of the Church's energies to a new evangelization and to the mission ad gentes (to the Gentiles). No believer in Christ, no institution of the Church can avoid this supreme duty: to proclaim Christ to all peoples."

"There is an intermediate situation, particularly in countries with ancient Christian roots, and occasionally in the younger Churches as well, where entire groups of the baptized have lost a living sense of the faith, or even no longer consider themselves members of the Church, and live a life far removed from Christ and his Gospel. In this case what is needed is a new evangelization or a re-evangelization."

St. John Paul II, pope
Redemptoris Missio: Encyclical Letter on the Permanent Validity of the Church's Missionary Mandate
7 December 1990

CONTENTS

Acknowledgments	vi
Preface	viii

PART 1: THE CALL   1

1	God Exists, Guaranteed - From Atheist to Believer	3
2	A Spiritual Pandemic Affecting the Whole World	17
3	God Loves You Personally - Believe it and Live it	27
4	Lord, Will Only a Few be Saved?	43
5	Are You Trying to Live in a State of Grace?	53
6	Make God the Centre of Your Life - Time is Short	61
7	The Battle for Your Soul	71
8	Build Your House on Rock and Guard Your Dignity	77
9	Emotional, Mental, Physical, and Spiritual Health	89

PART 2: THE FOUNDATION   97

10	The Key	99
11	The Door	119
12	The Garden	127

PART 3: THE RESPONSE   135

13	How to Stop Worrying for the Rest of Your Life	137
14	Let God Change Your Water into His Sweet Wine	149
15	The Holy Mass and the Eucharist – The Summit	157

Acknowledgments

16	Prayer with the Heart, Especially the Holy Rosary	171
17	A Model and Structure for Daily Prayer	181
18	Not the Valley nor the Mountain, but the Plain	193
19	Persevere, Persevere, Persevere!	203
20	Seek Fellowship with Other Christians	213
21	Be a Part of the New Evangelization	217
Conclusion – Putting it all Together		229
How Times Have Changed		235
Results of Spiritual Survey – May 2020		239
The Author's Conversion Story		247
Bibliography		253
About the Author		257

Acknowledgments

I would firstly like to thank my heavenly Father for the many graces that He has given me throughout my entire life, even when I was not close to Him. Having unexpectedly lost my earthly father at age 15 and migrated to Canada at age 17, I always felt alone and without any support. Unknown to me, my heavenly Father was always there supporting me and picking me up when I fell. His Son, Jesus Christ, is my Lord and Saviour, and without Him, I would not even be alive to write this book. To the many inspirations and consolations of the Holy Spirit, I say thank You, Lord.

I would also like to thank and honour my Blessed Mother Mary, who has always protected me under Her motherly mantle and continues to this day to lead me ever closer to the heart of Her Son Jesus. To the 17 Saints whose intercession I seek every day of my life, I say thank you: St. Joseph, St. Anthony of Padua, St. Thérèse of Lisieux, St. Frances de Sales, St. Dominic, St. Rita, St. Jude, St. Thomas Aquinas, St. John Paul II, St. John the Baptist, St. John the Apostle, St. Peter, St. Paul, St. Jeremiah, St. Louis de Montfort, St. Faustina, and in particular, St. Francis of Assisi.

I would also like to thank those family members, friends, and parishioners in Canada and Trinidad who were instrumental over the years from my return to the Catholic Church in 1986 in supporting and deepening my faith life. In a special way, the 20 years of fellowship that I spent in our Cenacle group in Toronto, Canada that met every Friday at 8:00 PM at various homes, were instrumental in strengthening my prayer life, especially the praying of the Holy Rosary. I also grew in my knowledge of Sacred

Acknowledgments

Scripture, the Catechism of the Catholic Church, and various encyclicals of the popes, especially those of St. John Paul II.

Fr. Tom Lawson, OP, was my spiritual director for a few years, and I benefitted tremendously from his wisdom, insights, and guidance. I am thankful to Fr. Alan Mohammed, OP, for the hospitality extended to me at the parish of St. Ann's and for keeping the Perpetual Eucharistic Adoration chapel open 24 hours a day, seven days a week, so that we the parishioners could benefit from countless hours spent visiting Jesus in the Blessed Sacrament.

During the pandemic times when this book was written, a special debt of gratitude is owed to some heroic priests. Firstly, I would like to thank Bishop Malcolm Galt, C.S.Sp., (Emeritus of Bridgetown, Barbados) for his faithful praying of the Liturgy of the Hours and the celebration of Holy Mass every weekday morning at 7:00 AM at Fatima College, and Fr. Gregory Augustine, C.S.Sp., for celebrating Mass every Saturday morning at 7:00 AM. Thanks also to my former Principal at St. Mary's College, Fr. Anthony de Verteuil, C.S.Sp., and Fr. Anton Dick, C.S.Sp., for faithfully celebrating Holy Mass every Sunday at 7:00 AM. They may not realize it, but we the parishioners were starved for the Mass and the Eucharist for at least half of 2020 when we endured two separate lockdowns due to the pandemic. We had to settle for Mass online and spiritual Communion, but now we grateful to be back in our Churches and receiving the Sacraments.

Finally, I would like to say a heartfelt thanks to all those who reviewed the manuscript for this book prior to its publication, especially Bishop Malcolm Galt, C.S.Sp.

Preface

For what reader audience is this book intended? Well, if you are not sure whether God exists or whether He loves you, or if you have lost your way and have fallen away from God and would like to return to Him, or if you have struggled to grow in holiness and have not made much progress, then this book will definitely help you get started on your journey back home where you belong – as a member of God's family. I would also sincerely like our youth and young adults to read this book because many of you have not had a proper foundation in spirituality and do not comprehend how much God loves you.

There is a second reason I believe that God wants you to read this book. Halfway through writing it, I became a little discouraged and asked God in sincere prayer if He really wanted me to finish writing the book and if people would really benefit from reading it. I then prayed to the Holy Spirit to guide my hands to open the Bible on an appropriate passage to answer my question. Here is the Scripture passage that the Bible opened to: "I will take my stand at my watchpost and station myself on the tower, and look out to see what he will say to me, and what I will answer concerning my complaint. And the LORD answered me: "Write the vision; make it plain on tablets, so he may run who reads it. For still the vision awaits its appointed time; it hastens to the end—it will not lie. If it seems slow, wait for it; it will surely come; it will not delay" (Hab 2:1-3). I received my answer, and thus, I continued writing the remaining chapters of this book. I hope you will read them all and that they will guide and uplift you spiritually.

There is a third reason you should read this book, and it relates to the subtitle of the book: "Helping you find your way back to God and grow in holiness." During the time of writing this book (2020), the

Preface

world was in the midst of a global pandemic, and the run-on effects include a severe downturn in the world economy, social unrest, mental health problems from stay-at-home orders by various governments, Church closures, and the list goes on. I sincerely believe that God is asking every one of us to find our way home spiritually and grow in holiness before it is too late. Even if all of this unrest due to the pandemic dissipates in a year or two, your life of 70 or 80 years will come to an end one day (and sooner than you think). Then you will have to give an account of your life before God. This book can help you get right with the Lord before it is too late.

Before continuing, some words of clarification are necessary. Everything spoken about in this book, along with the advice provided as to how to draw closer to God in a loving relationship, applies to you and me. Am I living fully by the advice contained within the pages of this book? I make it my daily duty to try my best. When I fall short, which happens to everyone trying to live a Godly life, I make sure to avail myself of the Sacrament of Confession. I also do a nightly examination of conscience as the Church recommends we all do. I ask God to forgive me for the sins I committed that day, and I ask Him for the strength and wisdom to learn from each of my falls and to become a better Christian with each passing day. It would be best if you also did the same.

Do you have to be a Catholic Christian to read, understand, and benefit from this book? The answer is no. Even though a Catholic Christian wrote this book, Christians of other denominations can benefit from the practical advice provided in this book. Catholics will, of course, gain the most from reading this book. God-seeking people of other religions can also benefit from reading this book. Finally, one important group of people can benefit from this book, and that is atheists!

The Key, The Door, and The Garden

Yes, because I was an atheist from age 18 to 24 while studying high energy physics at Queen's University and the University of Toronto in Canada.

I was armed with two degrees in high energy physics, and yet I was so restless in my mind about the crisis I was experiencing in my life that I had not slept at all for two weeks. God in his mercy then gave me the sign in 48 hours or less that I had asked Him for on a Friday night in 1986 at 6:00 PM, and He did not even wait until Sunday at 6:00 PM – He gave it to me by Saturday at 2:00 PM!

Since that pivotal moment in October 1986 when my life literally changed overnight, I became a "revert" Catholic. I started attending daily Mass, praying the Rosary daily, and frequenting the Sacrament of Reconciliation. I moved back to Canada in May of 1987 and became involved in many lay ministries in the Catholic Church for approximately 20 years.

Your life, too, can take a turn for the better if you trust what I will share with you in the pages of this book. Some of this book's ideas and teachings are based on three private revelations by God to the author, and I can take no credit for them. They were undeserved and were revealed to me during three intense periods of searching, praying, and earnestly asking God for the solutions to crises in my life. God always answers our prayers in crises if we fall on our knees and beg Him for solutions to our dilemmas. In the Book of Hosea, we read: "Therefore, behold, I will allure her, and bring her into the wilderness, and speak tenderly to her" (Hos 2:14). In the Book of Jeremiah, we read: "You will seek Me and find Me, when you seek Me with all your heart" (Jer 29:13).

The three private revelations by God to the author came in 1986, 2006, and 2019. The first one in 1986 was mentioned above in the dream that I received when I went from being an atheist to a revert

Preface

Catholic. You can read about the details of this powerful dream in the last section of the book, "The Author's Conversion Story." The second one came in 2006 in Toronto, Canada, when praying earnestly about a dire situation in my Information Technology business and forms the basis of the chapter entitled "How to Stop Worrying for the Rest of Your Life." The third one came in 2019 after returning from a pilgrimage to Medjugorje, Bosnia Herzegovina, and forms the basis of the chapter entitled "The Key."

The changes in my life from these three revelations were so profound that one could only attribute the wisdom given to me in these events to God Himself. I am not stating this fact to create fame, sell more books, or lead to sensationalism. I say this to help you, the reader, benefit from the wisdom that God imparted to me in these three events. I sincerely believe that these revelations were not meant for me alone but to help others in their journey toward a deeper relationship with God and ultimately help them work out the salvation of their souls.

Trust me when I say that making it to heaven from this life is not easy, but it can be attained by anyone who desires it and is willing to put in the effort and persevere on the journey. Isn't an eternity in heaven with God and all the angels and Saints worth putting our best effort forward? Then come with me on this journey as I reveal to you The Key, The Door, and The Garden that will help you get started on your path toward heaven.

Finally, the three revelations by God to the author described in this book are private and are not being presented as anything other than that. The author submits to the authority and judgment of the Catholic Church in all matters pertaining to these revelations and the contents of this book.

The Key, The Door, and The Garden

Anthony Hadeed, M.Sc.
- CEO, YourLifePurpose Limited
- Servant of Jesus Christ through Mary
- Author of "Dare to Discover God's Plan for Your Life Purpose"
- Founder of the Walk of Faith for Youth Organization

PART 1: THE CALL

"But you are a chosen race, a royal priesthood, a holy nation, a people for his own possession, that you may proclaim the excellencies of him who *called* you out of darkness into His marvelous light" (1 Pet 2:9).

"For many are *called*, but few are chosen" (Mt 22:14).

"Therefore, brothers, be all the more diligent to confirm your *calling* and election, for if you practice these qualities you will never fall" (2 Pet 1:10).

1 God Exists, Guaranteed - From Atheist to Believer

One important group of people I hope will read this book are atheists. Yes, because I was an atheist from age 18 to 24 while studying high energy physics at Queen's University and the University of Toronto in Canada. I wish Stephen Hawking and Christopher Hitchens were alive to read this book, and how much I would like Professor Richard Dawkins to avail himself of the material in this book, especially this chapter. These men were/are prominent intellectuals who have tried to convince the world that there is no God. In Stephen Hawking's final book "Brief Answers to Big Questions," which was published posthumously on 16 October 2018, he states the following (erroneously in my opinion):

> It's my view that the simplest explanation is that there is no God. No one created the universe and no one directs our fate. This leads me to a profound realisation: there is probably no heaven and afterlife either. I think belief in an afterlife is just wishful thinking. There is no reliable evidence for it, and it flies in the face of everything we know in science. I think that when we die we return to dust. But there's a sense in which we live on, in our influence, and in our genes that we pass on to our children. We have this one life to appreciate the grand design of the universe, and for that I am extremely grateful.[1]

---

[1] Stephen Hawking, *Brief Answers to the Big Questions: the final book from Stephen Hawking* (Hachette UK, 2018)

The Key, The Door, and The Garden

I am about to disprove Stephen Hawking's assertion above and with extraordinary first-hand evidence. While attending St. Mary's College in Port of Spain in my teenage years, which was run by the Holy Ghost Fathers (i.e., Spiritans), I was a devout Catholic and tried my best to live by the teachings of the Church. Then, when I left to pursue my university studies in Canada, I was taught by many professors who were avowed atheists. I was also bombarded by a pagan university culture, quite different from what I was used to at St. Mary's College. After my second year at university, I had completely lost my faith. Finally, after seven years of studying high-energy physics, I was desperately searching for the meaning and the origin of life because science had started to let me down with unanswered questions about the Big Bang Theory. During a summer conference at Yale University in 1985, I asked a Nobel prize physicist such questions as "who" created the primordial mass in the first place and "who" made it go bang, but none of his answers satisfied me. In October 1986, I turned in desperation and asked God if He existed to show me a sign in 48 hours. I would not recommend that you do this yourself, as I look back now on how I put God to this strict test! But my quest was a sincere one, and God had mercy on me. In less than 24 hours, God answered me and gave me a dream in which He revealed Himself to me in three parts of the dream. That was more than 33 years ago from this book's writing, and my life has never been the same since.

I have provided my full conversation story at the end of this book in the chapter entitled "The Author's Conversion Story." However, I thought I would give you some of the details of that powerful dream from 1986. I was armed with these two degrees in high-energy physics, and yet I was so restless in my mind about the crisis I was experiencing in my life that I had not slept at all for two weeks! Many people told me that I needed God in my life to have peace and direction, but I kept resisting their suggestions. I told them that they were trying to get me to believe in God because I was in a weakened and vulnerable state. It was now a Friday in October 1986, and I had left work and went home to my bedroom in my mother's house. I closed the door and said to God: "I thought that science had all the answers to life, but I am not so sure anymore. If you exist, please show me a sign by Sunday at 6:00 PM, and I will believe!" Now, I shudder to think that I gave God such a strict request, but in His kindness and compassion toward me, here is what happened. I still did not fall asleep on that Friday night, but when Saturday came, I returned from work around noon and again went into my bedroom to try to have a nap. I finally fell asleep for the first time in over two weeks and had this incredible dream. The dream had three distinct parts to it:

- In the first part of the dream, I saw myself kneeling and weeping at the foot of this large throne with someone mighty seated on the throne. All I could see were the sandals on His feet. After a while of me kneeling and weeping there, the person on the throne put His hand on my shoulder and told me that I could stand up now. This experience signified the repentance part of my journey back to God and the Church.

- In the second part of the dream, I saw myself as a boy around age 12 years standing next to Jesus Christ. I could see His Sacred Heart in His chest illuminated by light, and I saw myself with a similar but smaller heart with light streaming out from it as well. We were standing together looking out on what seemed to be a vast multitude of people of all races, ages, religions, and even moral standings (good and bad people). But there was only one response that He felt toward all these people, and that was love. He invited me to have the same response to everyone. This second experience signified the mission of every Christian and human being, for that matter, to love others unconditionally as Christ loves them.

- In the third part of the dream, I saw myself in this huge deep pit standing next to Christ. There were many people at the top of this pit with shovels in their hands, and they intended to bury us in the pit. I turned to Jesus and said: "Lord, they are about to bury us alive in this pit – let us get out of here quickly." He said to me: "Do not worry, simply kneel next to Me and pray, and you will see that no harm will come to us." Reluctantly, I knelt next to Jesus and began praying. From the corner of my eye, I could see all these people picking up their shovels and filling them with dirt. They made the motion of wanting to throw the dirt into the pit, but miraculously, no dirt ever fell on us, just as Jesus had promised. Jesus taught me in this part of the dream that when a person tries to live a good Christian life, many enemies will try to destroy him or her, but by staying close to Christ in prayer, no harm will come their way.

In His mercy, God had given me the sign I had asked for on that Friday night in October 1986, and He did not even wait until Sunday at 6:00 PM – He gave it to me by Saturday at 2:00 PM! In the process, He also gave me a complete theology lesson in the three parts of the dream: (i) the need for constant repentance and conversion, (ii) living the Christian life means loving God and every single human being unconditionally, and (iii) the need to stay close to Christ in prayer to defeat one's enemies in the Christian journey. When I awoke from the dream, I immediately found the nearest Catholic Church and sought a priest for Confession. I confessed my sins for the six-year period when I had been away from the Church as an atheist. What relief and joy I felt at that moment, and still experience to this day when I go to Confession.

Since that pivotal moment in October 1986 when my life literally changed overnight, I became a "revert" Catholic. I started attending daily Mass, praying the Rosary daily, and frequenting the Sacrament of Reconciliation. I moved back to Canada in May of 1987 and became involved in many lay ministries in the Catholic Church for approximately 20 years.

Holiness or Sinfulness – Your Choice and Mine

Holiness leads to eternal happiness. Sinfulness leads to eternal sadness. Prayer leads to holiness, and a lack of prayer leads to sinfulness. You can take that as absolute truth based on over 2,000 years of Christianity and its teachings, based on similar teachings in other world religions, and from personal experience, yours, and mine. Now, allow me to provide some further insight into this age-old problem of how to achieve holiness in this life, whether you are a layperson working at a profession, raising a family at home, or living a religious life. In Jesus' own words in His Sermon on the Mount: "Blessed are those who hunger and thirst for righteousness, for they shall be satisfied" (Mt 5:6). In the First Letter of Peter, we read: "As obedient children, do not be conformed to the passions of your former ignorance, but as He who called you is holy, you also be holy in all your conduct, since it is written, "You shall be holy, for I am holy"" (1 Pet 1:14-16). If you are not at this very moment and for the remaining days of your life on earth, hungering and thirsting for holiness, then you will never achieve it. Start now, or you will live to regret it. Do not think for a minute that holiness is boring; it is the greatest undertaking you will ever embark on in your life.

All of us are called to holiness if we want to have inner joy and peace in this life, followed by a life of total happiness and peace when we pass from this world to the next. The author conducted a spiritual survey in May 2020, and you can find the full results of the survey near the end of the book in the chapter entitled "Results of Spiritual Survey - May 2020." It showed the following intriguing results:

- 85% of the respondents considered themselves practicing Christians or persons practicing another faith.

- 60% of the respondents said that they are both satisfied with their relationship with God and are ready to meet their Maker should He call them from this life tomorrow.

- 90% of the respondents spend less than a half-hour, and only 10% spend more than half an hour in morning prayer before beginning their day.

- 80% of the respondents spend less than an hour in total, and only 20% of people spend more than an hour a day in prayer.

- 75% of the respondents said that there are areas of their lives that they have struggled with frequently or on-and-off for an extended period that they just have not been able to correct. 85% of these respondents said that they would like to correct those areas once and for all.

- Finally, over 70% of the respondents said they would be willing to adopt a proven self-improvement method in their spiritual life and persevere until they saw tangible changes.

It is a little paradoxical that over 60% of respondents said that they are both satisfied with their relationship with God and are ready to meet their Maker should He call them from this life tomorrow. Yet 75% have unresolved struggles in their spiritual life. More than 90% do not spend enough time in daily prayer. The missing link for most of the world's population is the quality and quantity of our daily prayer. You read that correctly, quality *and* quantity. It is a well-known fact that prayer is food for the soul. We spend at least three hours a day preparing and eating our meals to feed our physical bodies. We would not prepare nice-tasting and healthy meals that were tiny in quantity, correct? Similarly, it would not be wise to prepare and eat lots of unhealthy junk food. Both of these mistakes would lead to a diseased body. The same goes for our souls.

It appears that we are deluding ourselves and have developed a certain degree of presumption in thinking that we are "right" with the Lord and are ready to meet Him. The good news that this book brings to you is this: there is a way for us to be prepared to meet our Maker anytime that He might call us to Himself, whether it is before this day is over or whether it is 30 years from now.

The title of this book should have piqued your interest, especially the first two words: "The Key." You and I possess the key in our hands to get into a better relationship with God, but we must use it to open "The Door," which leads to "The Garden." These three phrases are metaphors that God revealed to me after returning from a pilgrimage to Medjugorje, Bosnia Herzegovina, in 2019.

The Key, The Door, and The Garden

I have spent many long years since God gave me that incredible dream in 1986, trying to deepen my relationship with Him and trying to have that inner peace of knowing that I am ready to meet Him at any time. I want to spare you years of searching, rising, and falling in your quest to live a life of holiness. Recall that holiness leads to everlasting happiness and that sinfulness leads to sadness for all eternity. Would you like to have deep inner peace and joy? Then, you need to read the remainder of this book, and I promise that you will understand how simple and yet how profound is this Key that God has revealed to us in Scripture, but which sadly, many of us have never really grasped or lived.

In his book "The Four Signs of a Dynamic Catholic," renowned author Matthew Kelly mentions in chapter 2: "Here I think we stumble upon one of the greatest tragedies of modern Christianity, and perhaps Catholicism in particular. We do an awful lot of talking about prayer, but we spend very little time actually teaching people how to pray. We assume that people know how to pray, but the truth is when most people sit down in the classroom of silence to make an earnest attempt at prayer, they haven't got the foggiest idea how to begin."[2] Later in chapter 2, Matthew Kelly lists the seven steps of "The Prayer Process," which should take an average of ten minutes but is expandable or contractible. He also talks about the four signs of a Dynamic Catholic: prayer, study, generosity, and evangelization. I want to take the first area, namely, prayer, and delve into it a lot more comprehensively. While he strives to make Catholics more dynamic by getting them to practice the four signs, I would like to help you at least work out your salvation and eventually make it to

---

[2] Matthew Kelly, The Four Signs of a Dynamic Catholic: How Engaging 1% of Catholics Could Change the World (Blue Sparrow Books, 2014), 47.

heaven because that is not an easy proposition. God has given us a way and the means to get that process started and to persevere until it is complete. Then you can go on to trying to become more dynamic in your faith life.

In another of his books "Rediscover the Saints", Matthew Kelly states the following in chapter 5 "Teresa of Avila: The First Routine":

> Teaching people to pray is central to our mission as Christians. Everything good that we long for will be the fruit of prayer. Any worthwhile hope we have for ourselves, our children, our families, the Church, and the world will be the result of a chain reaction set off by prayer. Prayer sets in motion a domino effect of goodness.
>
> We learn to live deeply by praying deeply. Find that place within you where you can connect with God, and start to spend time in that place every day. Find that place within you where you can discover more and more about the-best-version-of-yourself. Make your prayer time a sacred item on your schedule. Make it non-negotiable.[3]

Here is the challenge that most people will have after reading the above advice: they will not know how to begin building and sustaining their prayer life. In my experience since 1986 of developing my prayer life to the point of being at peace with God and trying to live in His will, every person needs to give sufficient quantity and quality time to God before their day begins. The current book seeks to help you build a solid and sustainable prayer life that leads to holiness. It aims to show you what The Key is that leads to The Door, which opens to

---

[3] Matthew Kelly, *Rediscover the Saints: Twenty-five Questions that Will Change Your Life* (Blue Sparrow, 2019), 32-33.

The Key, The Door, and The Garden

The Garden, and it seeks to show you what can happen if you do not use The Key.

Here is a beautiful description of what prayer can do for your soul and its relationship with God. It was written by St. John Chrysostom (a name which means 'golden-mouthed' because of the eloquence of his sermons):

> Prayer and converse with God is a supreme good: it is a partnership and union with God. As the eyes of the body are enlightened when they see light, so our spirit, when it is intent on God, is illumined by his infinite light. I do not mean the prayer of outward observance but prayer from the heart, not confined to fixed times or periods, but continuous throughout the day and night.
>
> Our spirit should be quick to reach out toward God not only when it is engaged in meditation; at other times also, when it is carrying out its duties, caring for the needy, performing works of charity, giving generously in the service of others, our spirit should long for God, and call him to mind, so that these works may be seasoned with the salt of God's love, and so make a palatable offering to the Lord of the universe. Throughout the whole of our lives, we may enjoy the benefit that comes from prayer if we devote a great deal of time to it.
>
> Prayer is the light of the spirit, true knowledge of God, mediating between God and man. The spirit, raised up to heaven by prayer, clings to God with the utmost tenderness; like a child crying tearfully for its mother, it craves the milk that God provides. It seeks the satisfaction of its own desires, and receives gifts outweighing the whole world of nature.

When the Lord gives this kind of prayer to someone; he gives him riches that cannot be taken away, heavenly food that satisfies the spirit. One who tastes this food is set on fire with an eternal longing for the Lord: his spirit burns as in a fire of the utmost intensity.[4]

There are many orders and movements within the Church that laypeople can explore to deepen their relationship with God and solidify their commitment to following Him more faithfully. Such orders and movements include the Third Order Franciscans, Secular Franciscans, the lay Dominicans, the Opus Dei, the Society of the Little Flower of St. Thérèse of Lisieux, the Confraternity of Mary, Queen of all Hearts, and many more. I have explored many of these orders and movements since 1990 and have learned a lot from each of them. I am particularly drawn to Franciscan spirituality and to the type of Marian devotion as espoused by St Louis De Montfort in his famous book, "True Devotion to Mary." However, many people will never officially join and stay with any of these orders or movements. Yet all of us are called to lives of holiness and intimacy with God, our Creator. God is calling you and me to make it to heaven one day. If you feel yourself belonging to this group of people, this book will most certainly help you achieve it.

In her book "Single for a Greater Purpose," author Luanne D. Zurlo discusses at length a growing group of people within the Church, and that is, "dedicated singles." These are people within the Church who are single and celibate for the sake of the kingdom but who have not taken official public religious vows. Many of these

---

[4] St. John Chrysostom, bishop, *Supplement Homily 6 De precatione*, 64, 462-466

dedicated singles do not know how to structure their prayer life in order to remain faithful to God and to avoid sin, at least serious ones. Zurlo states in chapter 10, "A Needed Witness Today":

> Perhaps dedicated singles today may be able to play a similar role, helping those unable to respond to ordained priests or religious, whose clerical clothing, habits, and radical way of life may be too bright for souls unused to the light.
>
> Might the lights of dedicated singles, discretely twinkling throughout all walks of life, serve some special purpose in this historical moment that sorely lacks exemplary leadership?[5]

It may be the case that after you read this book, you will feel that the Lord is calling you to join one of the orders or movements mentioned above. Doing so would provide you with support and fellowship with other Catholic Christians who share the same passion for some specific charisms of Jesus Christ. I would encourage you to pursue that calling by contacting a representative from that order or movement that attracts you. Alternatively, you may feel called to start a prayer group based on the methods and model of prayer outlined in this book, and that would be great as well. The Lord will take your more sincere conversion and love for Him, whichever way He can get it and whichever way suits your personality. He is not a rigid God.

In a few of this book's chapters, I mention Our Lady of Medjugorje's apparitions in Bosnia Herzegovina to six visionaries reputed to have begun on 24 June 1981 and continue to the time of writing of this book. The author submits to the final decision of the

---

[5] Luanne D. Zurlo, *Single for a Greater Purpose: A Hidden Joy in the Catholic Church* (Sophia Institute Press, 2019), 144.

Catholic Church on the authenticity of these apparitions. On 11 February 2017, the Archbishop of Warsaw Poland, Henryk Hoser, was appointed by Rome as Papal Envoy to Medjugorje. In May 2017, the findings of the Ruini Commission were made public. The commission recommended the first seven days of the apparitions be approved and that Medjugorje be turned into a pontifical sanctuary. The commission made no recommendations about any of the apparitions which occurred after the first seven days. Archbishop Hoser made a point to invite all believers to go to Medjugorje, if they are able, and to receive spiritual renewal. "I would highly recommend it. I would say that it is the pilgrimage of spiritual change, conversion, and strengthening of faith – you can experience all of that there."

Summary

I have proven to you beyond a shadow of a doubt that God exists and that He is a loving and merciful God. The only reason you now have for not believing that God exists is that you prefer not to believe in Him; you know in your heart that accepting His existence will cause you to have to make many changes in your life, and you are not ready to make those changes. When you are ready, go ahead and believe. I have shown you what happened to me back in 1986 and how my own life took a turn for the better. Your life, too, can take a turn for the better, and most of all, you should not gamble with your eternal destiny by stubbornly remaining in your unbelief.

2   A Spiritual Pandemic Affecting the Whole World

Spiritual vs. Physical Pandemics

The world was caught off guard in late 2019 when the novel Coronavirus pandemic started to spread to all countries worldwide. It is safe to say that the world went into panic mode. There were border lockdowns, social distancing guidelines, the wearing of facemasks by entire populations, an economic downturn worse than the Great Recession of 2008, and a host of mental health problems caused by people's isolation in their homes. Most of all, the fear that has gripped the majority of people around the world is surreal! Indeed, the world has experienced pandemics before, as the following data indicates:

- 2019-today: COVID-19 pandemic (SARS-CoV-2 virus) has killed over six million people globally as of the publication of this book. When this pandemic hopefully gets under control, the global death toll may be upwards of seven million or more.

- 2009-2010: Swine flu pandemic (H1N1 virus) killed 284,000 people globally.

- 1968-1969: Hong Kong flu pandemic (H3N2 virus) killed between one to four million people globally.

- 1957-1958: Asian flu pandemic (H2N2 virus) killed one million people globally.

- 1930-today: the seasonal flu kills between 30,000 to 60,000 people annually.

- 1918-1919: Spanish flu pandemic (H1N1 virus) killed an estimated 50 million people globally.

- Tuberculosis (TB) is a global disease found in every country in the world. It is the leading infectious cause of death worldwide. The World Health Organization estimates that 1.8 billion people, close to one-quarter of the world's population, are infected with Mycobacterium tuberculosis (MTB), which causes TB. In 2019, 10 million fell ill from TB, and 1.5 million died.

These are some gruesome statistics that many people may not be aware of, which is why the fear factor surrounding the COVID-19 pandemic needs closer examination. We are continually being bombarded with daily statistics of an increasing number of cases and deaths, causing many people to panic. This fear is heightened by modern social media and global internet news access. Some have put forward conspiracy theories about the international power brokers using fear to try to control entire populations and even the world at large. Some have even suggested an apocalyptic dimension to the COVID-19 pandemic. I believe that some or maybe even all of the above explanations have a degree of truth to them (time will tell).

However, I believe that there are more profound reasons for the excessive amount of fear that people are experiencing today over this particular pandemic. Firstly, there is a saying that most people are familiar with: "Everybody wants to go to heaven, but nobody wants to die." This statement implies that everyone believes in a place called heaven and wants to go there, but people are afraid of the process and

A Spiritual Pandemic Affecting the Whole World

the pain of dying. From my observation over the past number of decades, I believe this saying should be updated to the following: "Everybody has stopped believing in heaven, and that is why nobody wants to die." But to truly live, we first need to die to ourselves. "For whoever would save his life will lose it, but whoever loses his life for my sake will find it" (Mt 16:25).

There is a term used in modern theology called "practical atheism" or "fluid atheism." This term is spoken of at length in the book by Robert Cardinal Sarah and Nicolas Diat, entitled "The Day Is Now Far Spent." In this book, Cardinal Sarah tries to show that fluid atheism is the common root of all current crises, which, without denying God, lives in practice as if He did not exist. He says in his concluding message:

> I think that our time is experiencing the temptation to atheism. Not the hard, militant atheism we have seen aping Christianity through Marxist or Nazi pseudo-liturgies. That sort of atheism, a kind of religion in reverse, has become discreet. I mean, rather, a subtle, dangerous state of mind: fluid atheism. Now that is an insidious, dangerous sickness, even though its first symptoms seem benign...
>
> We must realize that this fluid atheism runs through our veins. It never stays the same, but it infiltrates everywhere. And nevertheless, Saint Paul recommends: "Do not be mismatched with unbelievers. For what partnership have righteousness with iniquity? Or what fellowship has light with darkness? What accord has Christ with Belial? Or what has a believer in common with an unbeliever? What agreement has God with the temple of idols?"

(2 Cor 6:14-16). Despite the warnings of Saint Paul, we coexist fraternally and peacefully with fluid atheism; [6]

Suppose the majority of people in the world have inadvertently contracted this "virus" of fluid atheism. In that case, either consciously or subconsciously, people now believe that they are only guaranteed life on earth. This may be one of the underlying reasons for their fear of catching and possibly dying from physical viruses or other hidden enemies.

There may be a second reason for the excessive amount of fear, and that is widespread egoism. The Catechism of the Catholic Church states:

> Before Christ's second coming the Church must pass through a final trial that will shake the faith of many believers. The persecution that accompanies her pilgrimage on earth will unveil the "mystery of iniquity" in the form of a religious deception offering men an apparent solution to their problems at the price of apostasy from the truth. The supreme religious deception is that of the Antichrist, a pseudo-messianism by which man glorifies himself in place of God and of his Messiah come in the flesh.[7]

Pride is the original sin that Lucifer himself committed when he rebelled against God's absolute rule in heaven. He has been trying ever since to get man's pride and ego to swell to the point of his own

---

[6] Robert Cardinal Sarah, Nicolas Diat, *The Day Is Now Far Spent* (Ignatius Press, 2019), 334-335.

[7] *Catechism of the Catholic Church, Second Edition* (Libreria Editrice Vaticana, 1994, 1997), no. 675.

so that man believes either consciously or subconsciously that he is equal to God. Technological advancements and the exponential growth in knowledge accessible to almost anyone with a click of a button on the internet have led man to believe that he is invincible and will live for a very long time on earth. Then, along comes this virus that threatens man's existence, and panic and fear have set in.

There is a third reason for the excessive fear that the world is experiencing over the COVID-19 pandemic, namely, the "virus" of idolatry. We will explore this "spiritual pandemic" in the next section of this chapter but suffice it to say that "spiritual pandemics" are much worse than physical pandemics. The reason is that while a biological pandemic can end your life on earth, you can still end up in heaven for all eternity, enjoying happiness and peace with God and with all the angels and Saints. However, suppose you die and have a hidden "spiritual virus" within your soul. In that case, you will experience the exact opposite of eternal happiness and peace with God. You will experience eternal suffering with Satan and with all his angels and the souls of the damned. While we need to take the necessary health precautions against the physical pandemics, should we not be more concerned with "spiritual pandemics" in the world and to which we might have fallen prey without knowing it?

Idolatry Abounds Everywhere

In chapter 3, we will explore the various reasons for believing in the depths of our hearts how much God loves each one of us personally. The sad truth is that most people do not love God in return because they have become too busy to spare God a moment or two of their busy day. That is because many idols have crept into our hearts without us even knowing it. The world around us is continually bombarding us with things we should have, material things we should buy, activities we should engage in, fashions we should wear, and so on. While not looking outwardly like idols, these are nevertheless idols of the heart.

Why does God dislike idolatry so much? It violates the first of the Ten Commandments He gave to the chosen people on Mount Sinai through His servant Moses. Idolatry does more harm to us than we know, and when we substitute the proper worship due to God alone with the worship of people or things that cannot compare to God, we set ourselves on a path to breaking all of the other Commandments. In its short form, the First Commandment states: "I am the LORD your God, who brought you out of the land of Egypt, out of the house of slavery. You shall have no other gods before Me" (Exod 20:2-3).

Idolatry is the worship of other "gods" instead of the one true God. Now, we might think that we do not worship other gods in our time because we are not bowing down to a "golden calf," as the Israelites did in the desert when Moses went up the mountain to get the Ten Commandments from God; but the exact opposite is true. Never has idolatry abounded so much as in our time. Here are some of the gods that we worship: money, pleasure, power, ego, sports, sex, alcohol, drugs, gambling, celebrities, and technology in various forms such as cell phones, the internet, social media, etc. Of course, there are other false gods that we worship, but the above are the more common ones today.

Heaven is a place where each person loves God with all their heart, mind, soul, and strength. You can see that there is no place for idolatry in heaven. Those who do not go to heaven directly or indirectly after spending some purification time in purgatory will go to hell for all eternity, which is a terrifying proposition. The Catechism of the Catholic Church clearly states this:

A Spiritual Pandemic Affecting the Whole World

Death puts an end to human life as the time open to either accepting or rejecting the divine grace manifested in Christ. The New Testament speaks of judgment primarily in its aspect of the final encounter with Christ in his second coming, but also repeatedly affirms that each will be rewarded immediately after death in accordance with his works and faith. The parable of the poor man Lazarus and the words of Christ on the cross to the good thief, as well as other New Testament texts speak of a final destiny of the soul--a destiny which can be different for some and for others.

Each man receives his eternal retribution in his immortal soul at the very moment of his death, in a particular judgment that refers his life to Christ: either entrance into the blessedness of heaven-through a purification or immediately, -- or immediate and everlasting damnation.[8]

The people of Sodom and Gomorrah engaged in a type of sexual idolatry, and for this, God wiped out those two towns and practically all their inhabitants by raining down fire and brimstone upon them. Our times have become worse than Sodom and Gomorrah's time and worse than the time of the flood when God wiped out all of humanity except for Noah and his family.

It follows that since idolatry is so rampant in our time than at any other time in history, humanity's consequence is dire. When God sounds the final trumpet, and time on this earth as we know it comes to an end, it will be too late for us to repent of our idolatrous ways,

---

[8] *Catechism of the Catholic Church*, Second Edition (Libreria Editrice Vaticana, 1994, 1997), nos. 1021-1022.

which have led to us breaking some or all of God's other Commandments. Just look around at what is happening in our world today, and you will get the sense that we are on the cusp of significant instability and worldwide destruction on so many fronts. These include the destruction of the environment, the unstable sociopolitical climate, family instability, rampant immorality, and the various civil and religious wars in the Middle East and Africa. Russia, NATO, and the United States seem to be on the verge of a new Cold War.

It almost feels like we are living on borrowed time and that God's hand of justice is being held back by the fervent prayers of a minority of people in the world who have not succumbed to idolatry and who still give God the worship He deserves. But make no mistake about it; there will come a time when God has had enough with how people are treating Him and one another. No one knows the day or the hour when Jesus Christ will return, which will signal the close of this age and a separation of good from evil. But Jesus' words from Matthew's Gospel ring especially true in our time: "Immediately after the tribulation of those days the sun will be darkened, and the moon will not give its light; the stars will fall from heaven, and the powers of the heavens will be shaken. Then the sign of the Son of Man will appear in heaven, and then all the tribes of the earth will mourn, and they will see the Son of Man coming on the clouds of heaven with power and great glory. And He will send His angels with a great sound of a trumpet, and they will gather together His elect from the four winds, from one end of heaven to the other" (Mt 24:29-31).

Let us turn away from all the idols that we serve in our lives and ask Jesus Christ to come into our hearts and reign there as King. Let us allow Him to root out everything in us that is not of God, and we will experience the peace and joy that only God can give. How do we

A Spiritual Pandemic Affecting the Whole World

know what our idols are? It is easy because Jesus said: "Where your treasure is, there your heart will be also" (Lk 12:34). Holiness leads to happiness, while sinfulness leads to sadness - that is easy to remember. God will say one day: *Last call, everyone!*

Summary

There seems to be a spiritual pandemic gripping the world in addition to the coronavirus pandemic that started in late 2019. Idolatry forms the basis of this spiritual pandemic, fuelled by practical or fluid atheism, which consists of living as though God does not exist, and not only atheists act in this way. These are some of the false gods we worship today: money, pleasure, power, ego, sports, sex, alcohol, drugs, gambling, celebrities, and technology in all its various forms such as cell phones, the internet, social media, etc. Of course, there are other false gods that we worship, but the above are the more common ones. We need to turn away from these idols and learn to love God with all our hearts, minds, and souls, and to love our neighbour as ourselves. If not, when we die or when Jesus Christ returns to find us in this state of idolatry, the consequences will be dire.

3 God Loves You Personally - Believe it and Live it

There is a reason why people fall so easily into the sin of idolatry, which we discussed in the last chapter, and it has to do with our belief in God's love for us. I wonder how many people believe deep within their hearts that God loves them personally? Most people believe that if there is a God, He probably loves the world because if He did not, why would He have created it in the first place? You and I are a part of this world, and so we believe in a general sense that God loves us. The point I want to explore here is whether you know that God loves you so deeply that He knows how many hairs you have on your head, and more than that, He cares about every single aspect of your life all the time.

I want to illustrate my point by relating a true story that happened to me in Toronto, Canada, around 1991. In 1986, I had already returned to my faith in God, and I was back in the Church. That was after God gave me that astounding dream in answer to my question as to whether He existed. My mother and sisters had gone on a pilgrimage to Medjugorje, Bosnia Herzegovina, in 1988 and had brought back a book of Our Lady's alleged messages to the visionaries. I read these messages and felt something stir within me to start living what Our Lady had recommended for us to grow in holiness. She recommended daily Mass, daily Rosary, daily reading of the Bible, monthly Confession, and fasting on bread and water on Wednesdays and Fridays. These are known as the "five stones" that will help slay our "Goliath." With all of this, you would think that I felt confident that God loved me deeply. But alas, that was not the case! In 1991, I attended a "Life in the Spirit Seminar" at St. Patrick's Parish in Toronto. The first of seven talks was entitled "God's love,"

The Key, The Door, and The Garden

and I will never forget the question posed to us by the presenter John. He asked each of the fifteen of us who attended that night to ponder the following question over the next week before returning for the second talk in the seminar. He said: "Do you believe in the depths of your heart that God loves YOU personally?" He did not want the answer to come from our heads or from what we had read in the Bible or what we were taught in school. He wanted us to examine our innermost being to answer the question truthfully. In any case, he said that God already knew the answer and that we could not fool Him.

Off we all went that week to our respective jobs and daily activities until we returned the following Wednesday for the second talk. John promptly asked us all to gather in a circle to share our answers to the previous week's question. Something peculiar then happened. Approximately five of the fifteen people answered the question something like this: "I have absolutely no doubt that God loves me, and that He is always with me and looking out for me." I was not part of that first group of respondents. The remaining ten of us answered the question more or less the way I did, which was: "Well, if I have a good day where I do not commit any sins and where I do not think or say anything bad about anyone, then I believe that God loves me. Otherwise, I believe that God tolerates me or even worse, that He is angry with me."

John wisely thanked all of us for our honest answers, especially the second group of ten. He said that God would work with our honesty in the coming weeks to show us how His love for us was unconditional. Even if we fall on occasion, His love for us does not diminish. When we sin, He is even more compassionate toward us because we are like the lost sheep that He tries to seek out. I thought to myself in the second talk that it would be awesome if in six weeks from now, at the end of the Life in the Spirit seminar, when we were to be prayed over for a reawakening of the Holy Spirit, that I could believe what John had told us was true.

When the laying on of hands occurred six weeks later, something changed within me, and I knew for sure that God loved me personally! I was 29 years old at the time and had never felt that way about my relationship with God. The point of this story is that many of us (like the group of ten of us who answered the way I did) have been raised in very authoritarian families, and we grew up with an excessive amount of fear for God. To fear God in a reverential way is one of the seven gifts of the Holy Spirit. However, to fear Him as always being angry with us is not healthy or conducive to growing in a loving relationship with Him.

Now, it would be nice if the story ended there, right? Old habits die hard, and what is ingrained in us from childhood can take a lifetime to correct. That was the case with me. Over the years, I found myself slipping back into my old way of thinking about God's love for me. For example, I believed He loved me conditionally on my holiness, as opposed to unconditionally and always, even when I struggled to avoid sin. A good analogy is the sun – it shines on us all the time, and even if clouds appear to block the sun or if we hide in our homes or a closet, it does not stop the sun from shining. That is the same with God's love – it is always "shining" on us to bring us His warmth and healing.

You may find yourself relating to me in terms of the ebb and flow of your deep belief in God's love for you personally. It most probably relates to the type of family you came from, as well as your personal life experiences. Here is something that has helped me and will likely help you as well; theologians have said that if you or I were the only sinners who ever lived, God would still have sent His Son Jesus to die on the cross for you or me. Does that sound too far-fetched? Well, it is not. Let us reason our way through this using science and mathematics to understand why this is most certainly true. If God were to say: "It's only one sinner, so why should I send My Son to suffer and die to save just that one person?" This would imply that God's love, while undoubtedly vast, had some limits to it. In other words, God's love would not be infinite. Then, we could conceive of another being whose love would be greater than God's love because this other being would be willing to suffer and die for just one sinner. Impossible right? This would make that being greater than God, which, by very definition, is not possible. You see, God is infinitely everything good. He is infinitely wise, knowledgeable, powerful, beautiful, and loving. Yes, you read that correctly. God is infinitely loving, and therefore if you or I were the only sinners ever to have lived or ever will live, then He would have sent His Son to suffer and die on the cross to save us! That is how much God loves every person on the face of this earth, and that is how much God loves YOU personally.

The Famous Gospel Passage – John 3:16

We have all read and even seen at sporting events the famous Scripture passage from the Gospel of John: "For God so loved the world, that He gave His only Son, that whoever believes in Him should not perish but have eternal life" (Jn 3:16). Now, I wonder what percentage of people, after reading that passage, come away with the firm belief that God loves them unconditionally? I will make an educated guess that it is less than 10%, and therein lies the problem with our world. If only we can believe that God loves us personally with an everlasting love, we would all be so much happier and less prone to sin, addictions, and idolatrous behaviour.

It helps if you substitute the word 'world' in John 3:16 with your name to get a better and more personal meaning of that Scripture passage for you. For example, if your name is Martin, then it should read as follows: "For God so love me (Martin), that He gave His only Son, that if I believe in Him, I will not perish but have eternal life." If your name is Suzan, then it should read as follows: "For God so love me (Suzan), that He gave His only Son, that if I believe in Him, I will not perish but have eternal life." I sure hope you get my point because this is how God dearly wants you and me to read that Scripture passage. I think you can also guess what the enemy (Satan) wants you to do with that Scripture passage - either you not read it at all, read and forget it, or if you do read and remember it, simply think that it is a general love for humanity but not for you personally. Whatever you do, Satan would not want you to come away believing in the depths of your heart that God loves you so much that He sent His Son Jesus to die just for you, as we discussed earlier in this chapter.

We must often remind ourselves that Satan's original temptation to Adam and Eve in the Garden of Eden was to get them to doubt God's love for them personally. He made them believe that God was not telling them the whole truth and that He could not be fully trusted in what He had advised them regarding which fruit to avoid eating. In disobeying God's advice to them, Adam and Eve essentially disbelieved God's love and concern for them, and they believed the devil instead. What an insult to God! Unfortunately, when we doubt God loves us personally, we too believe the devil's lie and are insulting God. I often remind myself of this stark reality when I am tempted not to believe that God loves me personally. You should do the same and repeat John 3:16 to yourself in a personal way as often as the enemy tries to make you believe that God does not love you personally.

The Greatest Promise Ever Made

Not only does God love every human being personally, but He also made the greatest promise ever to each of us through Jesus Christ. This promise was recorded in the last line of Matthew's Gospel: "And behold, I am with you always until the end of time" (Mt 28:20). He made this amazing promise just before He ascended into heaven. They were His last recorded words while He was on earth. He wanted us to remember and live these words every minute of every day. Why? Because He loves us immensely, more than we can imagine! Let us analyze each of Jesus' words to get the full meaning of His promise to each of us individually.

What does the English word "Behold" mean in the context in which Jesus used its equivalent in Aramaic? The word "behold" usually has been retained as the most common translation for the Hebrew word "hinneh" and the Greek word "idou." Both words mean something like, "Pay careful attention to what follows because this is important!"

Jesus says, "I am with you." Therefore, He is not delegating this job to someone else (e.g., an angel). He promised to be with you Himself. The Son of God, through whom the whole universe was created, is with you and with every one of us. He ascended into the spiritual dimension, which surrounds and permeates all of space and time. Thus, He no longer has the limitation of space and time and can be with everyone all the time.

Jesus says I "AM" with you. He does not say I will be with you, or I might be with you, or I am considering being with you, etc. He says that starting right now, I am with you, period. There is a double meaning here, too: "I AM" was the name God gave Himself when Moses asked His name, and Jesus also said, "Before Abraham ever was, I AM." In other words, Jesus, who is God, has been with you/us from birth to NOW. What a great and comforting thought.

Jesus says I am "WITH" you. He does not say I am at a distance watching you, or I am above you, or I am far away from you, etc. He uses the word "with" to signify that He is right beside you, you might say, glued to your side. He is with you wherever you go – at home, at work, at play, in happy and sad times, in life, and death. How much closer can He get to you?

Jesus says I am with "YOU." He does not say I am with your family or with your community, or with your grandmother. He says that I am with you, personally. He cares intimately about you (as well as everyone else). He knows exactly how many hairs you have on your head right now.

Jesus says I am with you "ALWAYS." He does not say I am with you sometimes, or I am with you most of the time, or I am with you when I am not busy, etc. He does not belong to a union, so He does not limit His time to 5 days a week, 8 hours a day. He says that I have the time to be with you always because I am God and I own time. I am with you seven days a week, 24 hours a day, period.

Jesus says I will be with you always "UNTIL THE END OF TIME." He does not say I will be with you always until you retire or until you turn 65. He does not say I will be with you always until the last of My disciples dies. That is why we know He was not only speaking to His disciples because they have all passed away, and time still exists. He was also speaking to souls alive today (like you and me), and to souls that will be alive in the future when He comes.

The Key, The Door, and The Garden

You are not alone, my friend, and you are not an orphan. You are not worthless or uninteresting, no matter what others say. You are so unique and lovable that the Son of God is with you seven days a week, 24 hours a day. Turn to Him now and say: "Hello Jesus. I love you, and I know that You love me." Talk to Him all the time in your own words – let people think you are crazy for talking to your invisible Friend. Tell them that they are the crazy ones not to speak with Him all the time.

Incidentally, this great promise of Jesus is most acutely fulfilled in the Blessed Sacrament because Jesus is present Body, Blood, Soul, and Divinity in the Eucharist, as well as in every tabernacle and adoration chapel in the world. He is truly Emmanuel, which means "God with us." Recall the story in Luke's Gospel about the two discouraged disciples walking along the road to Emmaus after Jesus was crucified. They were conversing with the stranger who had joined them as they walked along but whom they did not recognize as the risen Jesus: "So they drew near to the village to which they were going. He acted as if He were going farther, but they urged Him strongly, saying, "Stay with us, for it is toward evening and the day is now far spent." So, He went in to stay with them. When He was at table with them, He took the bread and blessed and broke it and gave it to them. And their eyes were opened, and they recognized Him" (Lk 24:28-31). We see clearly from this story that the two discouraged disciples immediately recognized Jesus when He changed the bread into His Body. That same Jesus is present in all the tabernacles and adoration chapels around the world. Do not leave Him alone but visit Him often and talk to Him about anything you wish.

God Loves You Infinitely More Than You Love Your Pet

Believe me when I tell you that the title of this subsection can help you believe how much God loves you. I know this from personal experience, and I am sure that many readers will relate to the following story. I owned a white Maltese dog in Canada whom I named Timmy. He was an affectionate dog but also very sickly. He required lots of veterinary attention, which cost a lot of money over his almost eight-year life span. However, you could not find a more loving and gentler dog, and he was a great companion for the time that I had him. Unfortunately, all of his medical conditions got the better of him. One month shy of his eighth birthday in June 2009, his occasional seizures took a frantic turn for the worse, and after five massive seizures in a row that day, he went blind, and the vet advised me to have him put down. The process took less than ten seconds, and little Timmy was gone. I am not ashamed to admit that I cried on and off for the year that followed, and I still have his ashes in a small urn by my bedside. In the moments when I sometimes doubt God's love for me personally, I hear the gentle voice of God inside of me saying: "I love you more than a million Timmys." God also reminds me that I did not create Timmy – I simply purchased him from a breeder. He next reminds me that He made me and that I am worth way more to Him than a dog. How can I then argue with God about that logic? You, too, must use analogies like this in the moments when you doubt whether God loves you personally.

Another story will help illustrate my point regarding learning from the care that humans give to animals and how much greater is God's love for His dear children on earth. I once watched a short video clip of a mangy dog who was all skin and bones and was dying on the streets of a town in the Philippines. A vet worker saw the dog, had compassion for it, and took it to his clinic to save its life. It took months of intravenous drips, medications, slow feeding, and careful body and skincare to nurse this almost dead dog back to life and health. A few months later, the dog looked normal and was even seen running around the compound, playing with the other dogs. Vets, who are fallen human beings, can do that for a mangy, almost dead dog whom they did not create; how much more can God take a "mangy," "disabled," and "abandoned" human being whom He created in His image and likeness, and nurse it back to spiritual health? No matter what sins you have committed in your life and for how long you have been committing those sins, God's love for you is infinitely greater than those vets' love for that mangy dying dog. Allow Him into your heart and experience His love for you. Sin will no longer be attractive to you because you will have discovered the only sure source of joy and peace in the universe: knowing in the depths of your heart that God loves you personally.

Jesus Thirsts for Your Soul

One of the seven last words that Jesus spoke on the cross was "I thirst" (Jn 19:28). If you recall that Scripture passage, Jesus was given vinegar to drink when he said: "I thirst." Now, I am sure Jesus was physically thirsty, but there was a symbolic meaning behind what He said. He was in effect saying: "I thirst for your soul; I thirst for a relationship with you." It is well worth your while to read the entire letter written by St. Teresa of Calcutta entitled: "I Thirst For You." The whole letter can be read (along with many other great prayers and meditations when visiting Jesus in the Blessed Sacrament) in the booklet entitled "All I ask is That You Love Me – An Adoration Companion."[9]

Look at what the guards gave Him to drink: a sponge dipped in vinegar, placed on a hyssop stick, and raised to His lips. I am sure His lips and mouth were parched with thirst. Yet, that is what He was given to drink in His thirst. What cruelty the soldiers committed towards Jesus while He was suffering. But this is the same thing we do to Jesus when He says to us: "I thirst for your soul, for a personal, loving relationship with you." Do we respond with love, or do we ignore Jesus? We often symbolically pour vinegar onto a sponge and hold it to His mouth and say: "Lord, drink this."

We often ignore Him and spend our time doing so many other things that are not of significant consequence to our souls and do not benefit our neighbour and the world. Is this what we should offer Jesus? Let us recall another Scripture passage when Jesus was dialoguing with a Samaritan woman at the well. He also said to that woman that He was thirsting, and He asked her to give Him a drink. There was a dialogue that ensued between the two that was quite interesting. As it turned out, we see again that Jesus was not just physically thirsty; it was a spiritual thirst, a thirst for saving souls. In this case, Jesus was interested in saving her soul. It was also about her conversion. Here is a part of the dialogue: "Jesus said to her, "Go, call your husband, and come here." The woman answered him, "I have no husband." Jesus said to her, "You are right in saying, 'I have no husband'; for you have had five husbands, and the one you now have is not your husband. What you have said is true" (Jn 4:17-18). We see that Jesus was conversing with this woman, who already had five

---

[9] *All I ask is That You Love Me – An Adoration Companion* (Medjugorje Herald, C/o iSupply Ltd), 87-97.

husbands, and she was currently living in an adulterous relationship. Despite that fact, her soul meant so much to Jesus.

What does that tell us? Regardless of the state of your soul and no matter what sins you have committed, Jesus is thirsting for your soul to be saved, period. In essence, He is thirsting for a personal relationship with you and me. But what do we give Him in return? Do we give Him our love? Do we give Him our fidelity? Vinegar is like our neglects, our infidelity, and our hardness of heart. Let us take Jesus at His word when He says to us: "I thirst for your soul; I thirst for a personal, loving relationship with you." I guarantee that you will never be disappointed. There is a line in the Liturgy of the Hours that reads: "Those who welcome the Word as the guest of their hearts will have abiding joy." Isn't abiding joy what you and I want? Let us respond to Jesus with love and fidelity, and open our hearts to Him throughout the day and invite Him in. Ask Jesus to be the guest of your heart today, and you will enter into a deep and loving relationship with Him that will bring you abiding joy, and at the same time, will quench Jesus's thirst for your soul.

You Are an Only Son or Only Daughter

There is an essential aspect of God's love for you that you must understand or at least accept. God treats you like you are His only son or daughter and as though there is no other son or daughter to whom He has to give His time. Does this sound too good to be true? Well, it is definitely too good to be true when it comes to our earthly parents or friends. That is because of our limited human mature. However, you must remember that God is infinite and can give Himself entirely and devotedly to each human being on the face of this earth, without diminishing His power by one iota.

Here are some essential facts that I believe are not coincidental and that God deliberately designed to help us understand and accept how special each one of us is to Him:

- Jesus is the only Son of His Father.

- Jesus was the only son and child that Mary ever had. She was a virgin at His conception and remained a virgin all Her life.

If Jesus enjoyed the above two privileges, why would God not extend that same privilege to us? If He only had limited time for each of us, we could complain to Him and say that we are not as fortunate as His own Son Jesus was in heaven and while He lived on earth. God would not permit us to have that complaint against Him. Similarly, Mary has been given the power by God to treat each one of us as if we were the only child that She has to give Her time two. Remember, some of the Saints in the history of the Catholic Church were given the power of bilocation, which means having the ability to be in two places simultaneously. Indeed, God has extended that same power but in an extraordinary way to the Blessed Virgin Mary. She can be with each one of us simultaneously and can listen to our needs and concerns. God, of course, has this power infinitely.

Here comes a bold statement: we must see ourselves in the above roles (God's only son or daughter, Jesus's only brother or sister, and Mary's only child). Otherwise, we will fall into the sin of pride and independence from God. We will think that God has only a limited amount of time for us, and then He has to move on to His other children. We will then feel that we have to live life and fight our earthly battles on our own, which is actually what most of us learned at home, in school, and the workplace and this is wrong. We must see ourselves in the above roles if we are to live Jesus' earth-shattering advice: "Truly, I say to you, unless you turn and become like children, you will never enter the kingdom of heaven" (Mt 18:13).

If God Loves Me, Why Do I Suffer?

We cannot conclude this chapter without addressing an important question that many people ask, and that is: "If God loves me so much, then why do I still suffer so grievously?" The answer to this question has two parts. Firstly, our suffering can be guilty suffering caused by our wrongdoings, which have natural consequences. For example, if I deliberately avoid paying the taxes that I owe the government, and an auditor discovers that fact, I will have to face the consequences of the law and may have to pay a fine. I may even have to spend a few years in prison, and this is guilty suffering. St. Paul reminds us that all sins have negative consequences when he said: "For the wages of sin is death, but the free gift of God is eternal life in Christ Jesus our Lord" (Rom 6:23). The fact that we experience guilty suffering does not in any way diminish God's love for us. Most times, God allows us to learn the hard way when we make mistakes or commit sins. The same applies to parents who do not place their children in a bubble. Parents allow their children to play and interact with other children, knowing that they will occasionally fall and hurt themselves. Nevertheless, they also know that their children will mature over time and hopefully avoid making the same mistakes in the future.

Secondly, our suffering can be innocent suffering, and this is the harder one to handle. However, I will give you a shortcut to deal with this – simply look at a crucifix and remind yourself that there was never a more innocent man that ever lived than Jesus Christ. The more life-like the crucifix is, and the more you gaze at it with reverence, the better you will understand and appreciate how much innocent suffering Jesus endured for us because of our sins. I have a life-like crucifix in my prayer room entitled: "I Am The Agonising Jesus Christ Who Loves You." There are scourge marks and blood all over the body of Jesus that sometimes brings me to tears when I pray the Rosary or Divine Mercy chaplet while meditating on the passion of Christ.

Innocent suffering has redemptive value, and that is why Jesus Christ, the perfect, spotless lamb of God, offered Himself in sacrifice to His Father for the sins of the world. St. Paul gives us a clue as to why Jesus' followers must also experience innocent suffering when he said: "Now I rejoice in my sufferings for your sake, and in my flesh, I am filling up what is lacking in Christ's afflictions for the sake of His body, that is, the Church." (Col 1:24). God the Father loves His Son infinitely, and yet He asked Him to accept the ignominious suffering and shame of a Roman crucifixion to save the world. In return, Jesus said yes to His Father and endured more suffering than you and I will ever experience. By the way, we are sinners, and so we should complain even less when innocent suffering comes our way because we can always offer it up as expiation for our sins and the sins of others.

St. Thérèse of Lisieux once said that Jesus shelters His friends under the shade of His cross and calls upon them to share in His saving mission for the world. Thus, when you find yourself having to endure innocent suffering, do not think it is because God does not love you that much and has abandoned you. Instead, reverse your thinking and say to yourself: "I am loved so much by God that He is calling me to follow in the footsteps of His beloved Son Jesus Christ." Believe that you will receive your crown of glory one day.

The Key, The Door, and The Garden

Summary

Only a small percentage of people in the world believe in the depths of their hearts that God loves them personally. God's love for each person is unconditional and unceasing. John 3:16 is a testimony to that. A good analogy is the sun – it shines on us all the time, and even if clouds appear to block the sun or if we hide in our homes or in a closet, it does not stop the sun from shining. That is the same with God's love – it is always "shining" on us to bring us His warmth and healing. One of the most incredible promises ever made to mankind is contained in the last words of Jesus Christ just before He ascended into heaven. He said, "And behold, I am with you always until the end of time." Let us believe that promise and accept within our hearts that God loves us personally all the time, even when we make mistakes.

He is always there to forgive us when we ask for His forgiveness, and He wants us to have a new beginning in our relationship with Him and with our neighbour, just like a mother is always willing to bathe her child, feed him or her, and help heal his or her wounds when they occur. A mother never counts the number of times that she has to take care of her child to make him or her happy. God is infinitely more loving and patient than the greatest and most selfless mother on earth. Jesus is most acutely present in the Blessed Sacrament in every tabernacle and adoration chapel in the world, so visit Him often and experience His love for you and His desire to be Emmanuel (God with us).

4 Lord, Will Only a Few be Saved?

Now that we know and hopefully believe in our hearts how much Jesus loves every one of us personally, does that mean that we will all automatically be saved and go to heaven when we die? I wish the answer were a simple "yes." The title of this chapter is not meant to scare you but to make you realize that, even though God loves us immensely and unconditionally, we cannot take our salvation for granted. If we do, we are likely to miss the mark, and we run the risk of being lost for all eternity. God does not desire that, but it would be due to our carelessness and apathy. Scripture reminds us: "For I have no pleasure in the death of anyone, declares the Lord GOD; so turn, and live" (Ez 18:32).

Jesus came to earth to show us the depth of the Father's love and mercy. What could be more merciful than when Jesus prayed on the cross to His Father for His executioners? In Luke 23:34, Jesus prayed, "Father forgive them for they know not what they do." However, make no mistake about it; Jesus is not one "big yellow daisy," as Fr. John Duffey in Toronto, Canada once remarked to a congregation. What did Fr. John mean by that statement? He taught us that we should not take God's mercy for granted and think that we can do whatever we want to in this life without repenting of our sins daily and without walking the path of conversion to become holier Christians with each passing day. Scripture warns us, "Do not be deceived: God is not mocked, for whatever one sows, that will he also reap" (Gal 6:7).

It is common in society today to think that nearly everyone will make it to heaven when the opposite may be the case. Scripture is full of passages that tell us that *God is merciful to those who fear Him*. "And His mercy is for those who fear Him from generation to generation"

(Lk 1:50). Those words came from the lips of Mary, the Mother of Jesus. One of Her titles is "seat of wisdom." In other words, of all earthly creatures ever created by God, She is the wisest of them all. Mary was also inspired by the Holy Spirit when She uttered those words as part of the Magnificat upon visiting Her cousin Elizabeth. Notice that She does not say, "His mercy is for everyone from generation to generation," but "His mercy is for those who fear Him from generation to generation." To fear God means to respect Him by trying to keep His commandments daily. When one falls short of the mark, one must recognize it and ask for God's forgiveness by making a sincere act of contrition. In the case of grave or mortal sin, try to avail yourself of a Sacramental Confession when a priest is available so that you can be fully reintegrated into the Church's sacramental life.

How many Catholics have not been to Confession in 10, 20, 30, or more years! This is a scary fact, given that we are all sinners and probably knowingly or unknowingly break one or more of the Ten Commandments fairly regularly. In his famous encyclical "The Splendor of Truth: Veritatis Splendor, Encyclical Letter,"[10] St. John Paul II, pope said that Christians should at a minimum be keeping the Ten Commandments. If they want to walk the path of perfection that Jesus invited the rich young man to do when he came to Him, then they should try to live the eight Beatitudes.

In "C.S. Lewis and a Problem of Evil: An Investigation of a Pervasive Theme," he talks about the phenomenon in modern theology about people claiming that they can read between the lines of Scripture. The text states on page 118:

---

[10] Pope John Paul II, *The Splendor of Truth: Veritatis Splendor, Encyclical Letter* (St. Paul Books & Media, 1993).

Lord, Will Only a Few be Saved?

Another way Lewis describes subjectivism as it presents itself in literary criticism is the phenomenon he calls "reading between the lines." Early in his life he developed a suspicion of this approach. As a young boy, he observed how often his father would guard a misunderstanding by claiming to have the ability to "read between the lines." Once the senior Lewis was convinced a truth was hidden or that somebody had a reason to hide it, any attempt to correct his error proved futile. He considered it a matter of cleverness that he could see what others could not.

Lewis' early skepticism of "reading between the lines" was reinforced by his experience as a student of philosophy while an undergraduate. In his autobiography, he writes that the tradition of Benjamin Jowett was still dominant at Oxford, and one was brought up to believe that the real meaning of Plato had been misunderstood by Aristotle and widely travestied by the Neoplatonists only to be recovered by the moderns. When recovered it turned out (most fortunately) that Plato had really all along been an English Hegelian.

It was this same practice of reading between the lines that led Lewis to question some of the work done by the higher critics of Scripture. They would miss the obvious but see the hidden, and Lewis reacted, "These men ask me to believe they can read between the lines of the old texts; the evidence is their obvious inability to read (in any sense worth discussing) the lines themselves. They claim to see fern-seed and can't see an elephant ten yards away in broad daylight!"[11]

---

[11] Jerry Root, *C.S. Lewis and a Problem of Evil: An Investigation of a Pervasive Theme* (ISD LLC, 2010).

The Key, The Door, and The Garden

There are many references in the Old and New Testaments that support the fact that not many will be saved. In the Flood, only eight people were saved (Noah and his family), along with a pair of every animal. In Sodom and Gomorrah, only a few people survived its destruction by fire and brimstone (Abraham, his household members, and his nephew Lot). Of the Israelites in the desert, Joshua and Caleb and their families were the only adults from that first generation who crossed over into the promised land. The remainder of the people who left Egypt died before entering the promised land because of their unfaithfulness to the Lord. The New Testament references below provide us with lots of food for thought about whether a minority or a majority of people will be saved and make it to heaven. I will leave it to your judgment, but please do not make the mistake that C.S. Lewis always lamented of, which is, "Do not try to read between the lines of Scriptures and forget to read the actual lines themselves." Here are some actual lines from Scripture to consider:

> "Not everyone who says to Me, 'Lord, Lord,' will enter the kingdom of heaven, but the one who does the will of My Father who is in heaven." (Mt 7:21)

> "If the righteous is scarcely saved, what will become of the ungodly and the sinner?" (1 Pet 4:18)

> "We must not put Christ to the test, as some of them did and were destroyed by serpents, nor grumble, as some of them did and were destroyed by the Destroyer. Now these things happened to them as an example, but they were written down for our instruction, on

whom the end of the ages has come. Therefore, let anyone who thinks that he stands take heed lest he fall." (1 Cor 10:9-12)

"Therefore, my beloved, as you have always obeyed, so now, not only as in my presence but much more in my absence, *work out your own salvation with fear and trembling,* for it is God who works in you, both to will and to work for his good pleasure." (Phil 2:12-13)

"And if those days had not been cut short, no human being would be saved. But for the sake of the elect those days will be cut short." (Mt 24:22)

"For many are called, but few are chosen." (Mt 22:14)

"Enter by the narrow gate. For the gate is wide and the way is easy that leads to destruction, and those who enter by it are *many*. For the gate is narrow and the way is hard that leads to life, and those who find it are *few*." (Mt 7:13-14)

Let us re-re-examine the last Scripture passage above, which are the very words of Jesus Himself. It does not get any more explicit than that. He says that most people take the easy road that leads to destruction (hell, to be precise), while the minority of people take the hard road that leads to life (heaven). Many theologians have said that we cannot tell for sure if anyone is in hell or actually goes there for all eternity. This assertion is a case of trying to read between the lines of Scriptures while ignoring the actual lines themselves!

I would like to humbly attempt to elaborate on the phrase of Jesus, "For the gate is narrow and the way is hard that leads to life, and those who find it are few." In the first part of His reply about how many will be saved, He says that many people take the easy way that leads to the wide gate, which eventually leads to eternal destruction. This means that it is there for the taking, and you do not have to go looking for it. Notice the change in action in the second part of Jesus' reply. He says of the hard way that leads to the narrow gate, which opens up to eternal life, that few are they who *find* it. We have to go looking for it to *find* it; it is not right there for the taking like the easy way. In reality, when we discover this hard way, fewer people take it because they realize how hard it is. Then, when those fewer people take the hard way, even fewer persevere until the end because they understand that it leads to their own personal Calvary, where they will have to suffer for the Lord before entering their glory in heaven as Jesus did. Along each of these filtering steps, the number of people who finally make it to heaven does not seem too great to me. Let us not water down Jesus' words and let us take the task of our salvation seriously.

The following is taken from a sermon on pastors by the great St. Augustine of Hippo, Doctor of the Church, entitled "Prepare your soul for temptation."[12] In his sermon, he discussed a common mistake among pastors entrusted to lead the flock, and this is to make the flock believe that it is easy being a Christian in this world. We all know the fallacy of the "health and wealth gospel" preached by many famous evangelists. Let us read St. Augustine's own words:

> But what sort of shepherds are they who for fear of giving offense, not only fail to prepare the sheep for the temptations that threaten, but even promise them worldly happiness? God himself made no

---

[12] Fr. Victor Abimbola Amole, *Words of the Fathers* (Lulu Press, Inc, 2015), sec. 31 (3).

such promise to this world. On the contrary, God foretold hardship upon hardship in this world until the end of time. And you want the Christian to be exempt from these troubles? Precisely because he is a Christian, he is destined to suffer more in this world.

For the Apostle says, "All who desire to live a holy life in Christ will suffer persecution." But you, shepherd, seek what is yours and not what is Christ's, you disregard what the Apostle says: "All who want to live a holy life in Christ will suffer persecution." You say instead: "If you live a holy life in Christ, all good things will be yours in abundance. If you do not have children, you will embrace and nourish all men, and none of them shall die." Is this the way you build up the believer? Take note of what you are doing and where you are placing him. You have built him on sand. The rains will come, the river will overflow and rush in, the winds will blow, and the elements will dash against that house of yours. It will fall, and its ruin will be great.[13]

Those are very sobering words from the great St. Augustine. To make it directly to heaven when a person dies, he or she must have achieved perfection in the eyes of God, living every virtue perfectly, and loving God with all their heart, all their soul, and all their strength, and loving their neighbour as themselves. Now, this is a tall order to achieve, even if we live to 100 years! The fact of the matter is that very few people make it directly to heaven when they die. If you are a living saint who has already achieved the perfection mentioned above, kindly provide us with your coordinates, and you

[13] Ibid.

would immediately be overwhelmed by visitors who want you as their mentor.

Luckily for the rest of us, there is a place in Catholic theology called purgatory where the souls of good people go (i.e., souls that are not yet perfect) to be completely purified and perfected before entering heaven. Finally, there is that third place that none of us want to end up in, and that is hell. In Dante's Inferno, there is a sign over the doorway to hell that reads: "Abandon all hope, ye who enter here."

Here are some quotes from C. S. Lewis' Screwtape Letters that illustrate the point of how smart the devil and his angels are and how much they want to lull as many souls as possible into hell with them. After all, misery loves company:

> Indeed, the safest road to hell is the gradual one—the gentle slope, soft underfoot, without sudden turnings, without milestones, without signposts.
>
> Screwtape reminds Wormwood that the present policy of hell's High Command is for devils to keep themselves concealed and invisible. This, he says, was not always the case, but it helps to make humans skeptics. One day, Screwtape hopes, people will worship the "forces" of science without believing in invisible "spirits." The modern image of devils as comical figures, Screwtape writes, will keep the Patient skeptical and, ultimately, help Wormwood corrupt him. Next, Screwtape considers whether to make the Patient a patriot or a pacifist. Except extreme devotion to God, he writes, all extremes are good for their cause. Because the Patient is afraid of the war, Screwtape recommends Wormwood try to make him a pacifist. The Patient may feel himself a coward, and, hopefully, become a hypocrite. But, if Wormwood decides to push patriotism, the objective is the same

to make the Patient think his cause is religious. As long as pamphlets and earthly causes mean more to the Patient than prayers and true charity.[14]

Summary

In concluding this chapter, I hope you now realize that it is hard to make it to heaven, and if you do not make it there, you might be lucky enough to make it to purgatory. Finally, if you are unfortunate enough to have not made it to either heaven or purgatory, then that only leaves one place, and that is hell. I pray every day in earnestness that every single person on the face of this earth will be saved and will make it to heaven or at least to purgatory. The sad reality may be something altogether different, so will you join me in praying daily and offering up your sufferings to the Lord to help save as many souls as possible from going the wrong way? God will reward you for all eternity. Remember Jesus' sobering words: "Enter by the narrow gate. For the gate is wide and the way is easy that leads to destruction, and those who enter by it are *many*. For the gate is narrow and the way is hard that leads to life, and those who find it are *few*" (Mt 7:13-14).

---

[14] C. S. Lewis, *The Screwtape Letters* (HarperCollins, 2001).

5   Are You Trying to Live in a State of Grace?

Do you know an amazing fact? If we were to ask the average person what it means to be in a state of grace, they would probably not be able to give you the correct answer. Pause and ask yourself if you know what it means to be in a state of grace before reading any further into this chapter. You might find yourself a little stumped. Yet, it is one of the most important questions a person can ask because it directly affects where they will go if they die today.

When St. Joan of Arc was asked during her trial if she was currently in a state of grace, she wisely answered: "If I am not, may God put me there; and if I am, may God so keep me." This statement came from the lips of a 19-year old French woman whose wisdom was beyond her years. Her answer teaches us that a person can never be confident if they are currently in a state of grace. Only God can know the exact state of our souls. Recall the information gathered from the author's survey, laid out in the introductory chapter of this book. We observed that approximately 60% of the respondents said that their relationship with God was a strong one and that they were ready to meet their "Maker," should they be called by Him from this life tomorrow. Unfortunately, most people's prayer life is not what it should be, and probably not like that of St. Joan of Arc. This observation from the survey indicates that, as a society, we have become somewhat presumptuous in assessing our relationship with God.

Mary is the model of a grace-filled person. The angel Gabriel addressed Her as follows: "Hail, full of grace, the Lord is with you" (Lk 1:28). The Church teaches that Mary was conceived without original sin (known as the Immaculate Conception). She never committed a single sin throughout Her life, even when She had to witness Her Son's crucifixion. Thus, She was full of grace at Her birth and remained full of grace for Her entire earthly life.

It is refreshing to observe the peaceful and joyful faces and internal dispositions of holy people in the world, such as living Saints, monks, nuns, and family men and women living holy lives. Conversely, the lives of more "worldly" people, such as some movie stars, professional athletes, actors, and musicians, are sometimes marked by addictions, marital infidelity, and mental health problems. Some of their lives even end in the tragedy of suicide.

So, what does it mean to be living in a state of grace? Fr. Michael Kerper, the pastor of St. Patrick Parish in Nashua, New Hampshire, and author on the Catholic Exchange, was once asked that same question by one of his parishioners. He replied in this way:

> Many people define the "state of grace" as the absence of mortal sin. Yes, grave sin is incompatible with the "state of grace," but this minimalistic understanding is akin to saying, "I've been hugely successful in life because I've never gone to jail." There's more to life than not getting convicted of crimes; and there's much more to the "state of grace" than avoiding mortal sin.
>
> To grasp the beauty of living in the "state of grace," we need a clear definition of "grace." Simply — and shockingly — put, "grace" is God! Allow me to refine this idea: "Grace" is God in that God freely communicates Himself to human beings, thereby enabling human beings to become like God. Grace actually transforms human beings into "gods" by adoption. This sounds bizarre, even heretical, but the New Testament boldly proposes this idea and many Greek-speaking Church Fathers spoke of the "deification" of human beings.

Are You Trying to Live in a State of Grace?

When God touches us through "grace" we begin to share in his qualities, one of which is immortality. Being in the "state of grace," then, liberates us from eternal death.

Now, let's consider the opposite condition: A person who falls out of the "state of grace" through mortal sin loses the necessary linkage with God and is necessarily excluded from the joy of eternal life. This seems horribly unfair, so we need to understand "mortal sin." This term refers to a free, conscious, informed, consensual decision to do something gravely wrong. It is a choice against the goodness of God.

Now, the question of how do you know whether you're in the "state of grace"? Frankly, we can never know this with absolute certainty. Nor should we conclude that any other person is not in the "state of grace."

While we can't have certainty, the regular practice of Confession is an enormous help. A frequent, thorough, and brutally honest examination of conscience will compel us to see habits, attitudes, and specific serious sins that pull us away from God's goodness, thereby possibly blocking God's life-giving grace. But, as I mentioned at the outset, the "state of grace" is not just the absence of sin; it's also the amazing opportunity to live fully as a "deified" child of God, sharing fully in God's life now and forever.[15]

Thus, the one condition that causes us not to be in a state of grace is the act of committing one or more mortal sins. If you are no longer capable of doing acts of charity toward your neighbour out of love,

---

[15] Fr. Michael Kerper, *What does it mean to be in the state of grace?* (*Diocese of Manchester magazine Parable, 2016*).

then you are probably no longer in a state of grace. You have essentially turned inward and are only looking after your own selfish needs and seeking after your own pleasures. The Catechism of the Catholic Church states this most clearly: "Mortal sin is a radical possibility of human freedom, as is love itself. It results in the loss of charity and the privation of sanctifying grace, that is, of the state of grace. If it is not redeemed by repentance and God's forgiveness, it causes exclusion from Christ's kingdom and the eternal death of hell, for our freedom has the power to make choices forever, with no turning back. However, although we can judge that an act is in itself a grave offense, we must entrust judgment of persons to the justice and mercy of God."[16].

Our Lady of Medjugorje once allegedly said to the world through the visionary Mirjana: "Dear children! As I look at you, my heart seizes with pain. Where are you going, my children? Have you sunk so deeply into sin that you do not know how to stop yourself? You justify yourselves with sin and live according to it. Kneel down beneath the Cross and look at my Son. He conquered sin and died so that you, my children, may live. Permit me to help you not to die but to live with my Son forever. Thank you."[17]

In our world today, sin is committed, justified, and therefore no longer confessed. That is a scary proposition, as attested to by the fact that most Catholics no longer frequent the Sacrament of Confession. One of the "five stones" recommended by Our Lady of Medjugorje is monthly Confession. We take a bath or shower daily to make sure our physical bodies are clean, but how often do we give our souls a

---

[16] *Catechism of the Catholic Church, Second Edition* (Libreria Editrice Vaticana, 1994, 1997), no. 1861.

[17] Medjugorje Message (https://www.medjugorje.org, 2 October 2009).

Are You Trying to Live in a State of Grace?

spiritual bath to cleanse them? In addition to monthly Confession to keep in a state of grace, the Church recommends a nightly examination of conscience. When you look back on your day and recognize the wrongs you may have done, in word, thought, and action, make a good act of contrition before you go to bed. In that way, if the Lord should call you during your sleep, you would have at least confessed your sins to Him.

Now we come to the crucial question: how do I avoid sin on a daily basis and remain in a state of grace? I guarantee you that you can try as hard as you want, but you will fail miserably. You better read that again. We do not have the strength to resist sin by our own efforts. Recall the words of Jesus: "Truly, I say to you, unless you turn and become like children, you will never enter the kingdom of heaven" (Mt 18:3). In the Letter of St. Paul to the Galatians, we read: "Yet we know that a person is not justified by works of the law but through faith in Jesus Christ, so we also have believed in Christ Jesus, in order to be justified by faith in Christ and not by works of the law, because by works of the law no one will be justified" (Gal 2:16).

What do these two important Scripture passages teach us about ourselves? They teach us that we must always have a humble mistrust of ourselves regarding what it takes to avoid sin. We must become like children as Jesus advises us. Whenever we see temptation coming our way, we must immediately call on Jesus, His Mother Mary, and our guardian angel to protect us from falling into sin. Otherwise, if we believe that we can fight and win the battle that has come upon us, we might very well sound like the Apostle Peter at the Last Supper when he told Jesus that, even if he had to die with Him, he would never deny Him. We all know that Peter had denied three times that he even knew Jesus an hour or two later! And imagine that Peter did this after witnessing firsthand Jesus' astounding miracles for over three years.

Now, an important point needs to be made here. The above advice about avoiding sin presupposes that we have absolutely no attachment to sin. We must also know that holiness leads to eternal happiness and that sinfulness leads to everlasting sadness. Sin always seems exciting when presented to us by the world, the flesh, or the devil. But when we sin, it leaves a bitter taste of guilt and separation from God and His grace. Look at what happened to Adam and Eve after they committed the original sin in the Garden of Eden. One can safely summarize the situation that ensued after they sinned with the famous phrase: "All hell broke loose."

There is another reason why some people find it hard to give up their attachment to sin – it involves emotional woundedness. According to John Bradshaw (the late American educator, counselor, motivational speaker, and author)- "All addictions have as their root cause, a shame-based core."[18]. Similarly, in his famous book "The Road Less Travelled,"[19] Psychiatrist Scott Peck said that in all of his years of treating people with various emotional disorders, he realized that the root cause of all of these disorders stemmed from the fact that the person experienced a lack of love growing up. That is such a sad but true observation, and it can cripple a person's desire to avoid sin and grow in holiness. If you feel trapped in the cycle of addictive sin, there is no shame in seeking emotional therapy and counseling. After all, when you have a physical ailment, you seek healing and even

---

[18] John Bradshaw, *Bradshaw On: The Family: A New Way of Creating Solid Self-Esteem* (Simon and Schuster, 2010).

[19] M. Scott Peck, *The Road Less Traveled: A New Psychology of Love, Traditional Values and Spiritual Growth* (Simon and Schuster, 2012).

medication from a physician. Too many people suffer silently (and often for decades) from emotional trauma through no fault of their own. This trauma then gets compounded by their inability to progress in their spiritual life. They go from feeling unloved in their early childhood to not loving themselves, then into marriages where they usually do not feel loved by their spouse (whom they may have chosen for the wrong reasons). Finally, all of this gets translated into not feeling loved by God. "Sin" is only too ready to receive such a wounded person into its arms and supply it with exciting "remedies" to lift its mood. But alas, we all know where this ends – in more misery. This topic is dealt with in more detail in the chapter entitled "Emotional, Physical, Mental and Spiritual Health."

Summary

To recap this chapter, a person can never know for sure if they are currently in a state of grace (like St. Joan of Arc's answer to the English tribunal). However, we can have a good idea that if charity is alive in us and we love others around us, we are probably in a state of grace. However, if we have turned inward by blocking out those around us and living only for our own selfish needs, then we have probably fallen out of the state of grace.

A reliable remedy for remaining in a state of grace most of your life is regular (monthly) Sacramental Confession. A bath or shower cleanses our bodies regularly and keeps them from becoming infected. Similarly, regular Sacramental Confession keeps our souls clean from serious sin and helps us to remain or get back into a state of grace. You most certainly want to die in a state of grace and not the opposite. The difference is most literally between heaven or hell and for all eternity! Please do not take any chances with your soul because eternity is forever! Always err on the side of caution - i.e., if you are unsure that you have committed any mortal sins, still go to confession, and unburden your soul to the Lord, through his representative, the priest.

6   Make God the Centre of Your Life - Time is Short

What would happen if someone decided to defy the law of gravity and goes up in an airplane to skydive without a parachute? He says: "I can break the law of gravity; I do not need to have the burden of a parachute. I want to skydive without a parachute. I want to feel free and do what I want to do. I want to skydive and enjoy the free fall, and I do not need a parachute. I am sure I can defy the law of gravity, and nothing will happen to me." So, he goes up in the airplane to twelve thousand feet, and he jumps out of the plane and starts skydiving.

Many other people like him jump out without parachutes on, and only a few people think that it is wise to have parachutes. The first group seems to be having more fun than the few people with parachutes because they are not burdened with parachutes on their backs. So, they are skydiving for quite some time because twelve thousand feet is quite a way up in the sky, just like seventy or eighty years of our lives may seem like a long time. They are skydiving and having a great time. They look at the people with their parachutes on, and they laugh at them. They are free and having more fun than them; life is more exciting for them up there in the clouds skydiving and doing what they want to do. They continue for quite a while, seemingly out of danger. But what happens to people like that? You and I both know that, while they think they are defying the law of gravity, in the end, they cannot break the law of gravity. They can only break themselves against the law of gravity. What happens to them finally? Well, their end comes quickly and disastrously when they fall and hit the ground without parachutes to brace their fall. We have all seen that happen so often with people who live ungodly lives - their end comes quickly and disastrously.

This same scenario is precisely what will happen to every one of us if God is not that at the centre of our lives and does not occupy the first place within our hearts. The sin of idolatry is something that every one of us can commit, and most people commit that sin in some form or another. Just because we are not bowing down to a golden calf as the Israelites did, does not mean that we are not practicing idolatry. Idols exist within our hearts - you can idolize sports, you can idolize money, you can idolize pleasure, you can idolize your house, your ego, you can idolize your job, your children, etc. There are so many things that we worship.

What do we need to do daily to make sure that we are in right relationship with God, that our hearts are right with Him and that we are not falling prey to the sin of idolatry? Remember the first of the Ten Commandments is: "I am the LORD your God, who brought you out of the land of Egypt, out of the house of slavery. You shall have no other gods before me" (Exod 20:2-3). If we do not keep the first Commandment, then how can we keep the other nine? All of us need to examine our hearts to make sure that we are not living idolatrous lives. We may think we are not, but on close examination, we probably are, in which case we are like that skydiver without a parachute. Our end can come quickly and disastrously too!

Let me give you a practical way to ensure that you do not fall into the sin of idolatry. However, before I do that, here is where the difficulty comes in. We have all inherited a type of disease from Adam and Eve, our forefathers. In the garden of Eden, their sin was one of pride and independence from God. They essentially said to God: we want to live life more independently. Does that sound familiar? I want to skydive without a parachute. Because we have inherited the sin of independence from Adam and Eve, we tend to live independently of God. But in Matthew's Gospel chapter 18, Jesus tells us: "Truly, I say to you, unless you turn and become like children, you will never enter the kingdom of heaven" (Mt 18:3). In the Letter of St. Paul to the Galatians, he reminds us: "we know that a person is not justified by works of the law but through faith in Jesus Christ" (Gal 2:16). When you put those two Scripture passages together, here is the disposition that you should have when you start your day, which the following prayer demonstrates: *"Jesus, my Lord, my God, my King, my Saviour, my Good Shepherd, my Brother, my Friend, my only Love, my Everything, I open wide the door of my heart to You. I humbly, sincerely, and lovingly invite You to come and dwell within me, to make Your home within me along with the Father and the Holy Spirit for You are all that I desire in the land of the living. I recall Your words and I know they are true: "Behold, I stand at the door and knock. If anyone hears My voice and opens the door, I will come in and dine with him and he with Me." See, a heart with a wide open door for You to enter if You so choose."*

This kind of prayer should mark the beginning of your day. You should remember throughout the day to renew this prayer to God. Now, that simple prayer should come from deep within your heart. You should mean it with every aspect of your being because Jesus is very sensitive to the sincerity of our invitation. If He detects within us any pride or independence left over from the original sin of Adam and Eve, and if He senses that we are not childlike in saying that prayer and that we do not mean it, then He will not enter us. Jesus is a passionate Lover, and He is looking for passionate lovers in return.

Try to pray that prayer throughout the day as you remember. God never forces Himself on us. He never assumes that if you invited Him this morning to live within you, that He is invited tomorrow or that He is invited this evening. Renew the prayer often – it is short but powerful. He is very respectful of our free will. God hovers over all the earth; He is present everywhere in nature. Whatever God has created, His spirit exists there. He can impose His presence anywhere, but there is one place that He does not force Himself, which is within a human being. God has created human beings in His image and likeness and has given each person free will. But He does not impose His presence within someone unless that person invites Him in. Now, when a person sincerely and lovingly invites God to come and dwell within him, then guess what happens? We know that God lives in heaven. The Lord's prayer starts: "Our Father who art in heaven…" So, God lives in heaven, and when we invite God sincerely to come and dwell within us, He accepts our invitation, and we become like a mini "heaven." Our souls become filled with God's peace, joy, grace, strength, wisdom, and power. We are filled with His light because God the Father, God the Son, and God the Holy Spirit, the Trinity, is now dwelling within us. We genuinely become temples of God.

You might ask: "What gets a person to the point where he or she can be sincere in praying that prayer?" I use the word "capitulation" – it is where we wave the white flag. It is like the alcoholic when he is "healed" by finally admitting that he will always be attracted to alcohol and is powerless over it. But he also realizes that there is a higher being, God, who has power over his particular weakness, and however often he calls upon Him, God will always come and help him resist taking that drink. The alcoholic knows that this will be his life for his remaining years on earth and that he will never get rid of his attraction to alcohol and become independent of his weakness. In some way, one might say that his alcoholism is a "gift" if he gets to the point of capitulation, of waving the white flag, of saying: "Lord, I give up. I lose this battle, and You win."

Make God the Centre of Your Life - Time is Short

Each one of us has a thorn in the flesh. St. Paul talks about this - there is a passage of Scripture in 2 Corinthians chapter 12, where he prayed and asked God to take his thorn in the flesh away. We do not know what it was. He struggled with some weakness, and he wanted God to take away the thorn in his flesh. Three times he prayed for God to remove the thorn in his flesh. But God said: "My grace is sufficient for you, for my power is made perfect in weakness" (2 Cor 12:9). Then St. Paul goes on to say: "For when I am weak, then I am strong" (2 Cor 12:10). St. Paul teaches us that we must get to the point with our weakness, where we accept that weakness as a "gift" and that we will always have it, just like the alcoholic. However, it does not have to destroy us or make us sin. What we essentially must do is to give up fighting on our own, give up our independent attitude that we have inherited from Adam and Eve, and wave the white flag. *We must become humble, and that is the exact purpose of our weakness.*

We have now put on the parachute so that when our lives come to an end, we will gently land in heaven. Contrast this with the person without the parachute who does not invite God to be at the centre of their life. That person's end will come quickly, disastrously, and permanently in the sense that his suffering will be for all eternity. Think of the analogy of the skydiver who falls and crashes to the ground but does not physically die. His bones are broken, and his skin is lacerated. He ends up in the hospital, and the doctors cannot do anything to alleviate his suffering. He is there for the rest of his life, suffering from all these pains. Think of that multiplied by millions upon millions, and that is what will happen to the soul that ends up in hell, suffering all the torments of hell in agony because he or she did not wear the parachute throughout their life. They practically lived independently of God, and they had a lot of fun and had many idols that they did not even know they had. But when their end comes, and it comes quickly, their suffering will be for all eternity.

Here is also something profound and unfortunate. Most people do not invite God sincerely to come and live within them daily. Most people are like the skydiver without the parachute. Only some people ask God freely, lovingly, and regularly to live within them daily. If you think I am exaggerating, Scripture backs up what I am saying. Remember the Scripture passages quoted in the previous chapter: in Matthew's Gospel chapter 7, Jesus says: "Enter through the narrow gate. For wide is the gate and broad is the way that leads to destruction, and many enter through it. For the gate is narrow and the way is hard that leads to life, and those who find it are few" (Mt 7:13-14). Again, in the Letter of St. Paul to the Philippians chapter 2, he says: "Work out your salvation with fear and trembling" (Phil 2:12). In the first Letter of St. Peter chapter 4, he says: "If the righteous is scarcely saved, what will become of the ungodly and the sinner?" (1 Pet 4:18). The New Testament implies that not many souls will be saved. This implication makes sense because how many people can you say regularly make God the centre of their lives daily? Not many people, and so most people are like the skydiver without the parachute - having fun but living idolatrous lives and breaking the first Commandment. Therefore, their end will be swift, their destruction will be permanent, and their suffering will be for all eternity.

I hope you understand the urgency of this message. We must put on the parachute, which is God's constant help. I hope you will take the practical advice given here and invite God daily to come and live within you. Mean it sincerely and know like the alcoholic that you do not have power over your thorn in the flesh. Whatever your weakness is, wave the white flag and become like a child. Turn to Jesus and say:

"Lord, You are the only one who can help me, the only One who can save me. Come and live within me." Then we can say as like St. Paul in his Letter to the Galatians chapter 2: "I have been crucified with Christ. It is no longer I who live, but Christ who lives in me. And the life I now live in the flesh I live by faith in the Son of God, who loved me and gave himself for me" (Gal 2:20). This attitude of complete dependence on God is our only hope to make it to heaven.

Before the Clock Strikes Midnight

Tick tock goes the clock of your life.
Is it filled with peace, or is it filled with strife?
Have you given your life yet to Him,
Or is the light within your heart growing dim?

He has said: "I am the Way, the Truth and the Life,"
Yet many ignore these words and live on the edge of a knife.
When will we come to see that this is utter madness,
Because to live a life without Jesus Christ leads to sadness!

As the clock of our life continues to tick,
We sit in darkness, and our soul becomes sick.
We try everything this deceitful world offers,
But to the way of life God shows us, we are scoffers.

Somehow, deep down within,
We know we are not living a life without sin.
We search for joy and peace to no avail,
And the day is fast approaching when our pleasures will fail.

He has said to us, come to Me that you might have life and light,
But we listen in disbelief and then live by our own might.

The Key, The Door, and The Garden

As the clock of our life approaches the midnight hour,
We continue to struggle by our own power.
Yet, the answer has always been so easy.
He has said to all those who labour: "Come to Me."
Are you sure that your life is grounded in Him,
Or are you careless with your soul while your light is going dim?

Those who build their house on Him are building it on rock;
They will gladly open the door when He comes with a knock.
Those who do not build their house on Him, build it on sand,
And the raging storms of life they cannot withstand.

What are you waiting for, my friend,
For another fork in the road or another bend?
For what if this is the last portion of your life's path?
You may not have a chance to cleanse in His mercy's bath.

You will reach the throne of God full of sorrow and regret,
For not having given your life to Christ when there was time yet.
Let this be an urgent call to everyone, small and great,
Come to Jesus Christ before it is too late!

The clock of your life is going tick-tock, tick-tock,
Wouldn't it be nice to be part of His faithful flock?
A great reward awaits you in heaven,
So, fill your life with Christ as bread is raised with leaven.

The clock of my life is fast approaching midnight.
I must be on my way to continue to live in His light.
No one's destiny in the afterlife is guaranteed,
But the best chance we have is to hasten to Christ with speed.

Anthony Hadeed
November 2018

Summary

Just like you cannot defy the law of gravity and remain unharmed when you fall from a high place, you also cannot negate the laws of God and have your soul not suffer the eternal consequences. While it might seem that you and others you know have defied God's laws for many years, this is only a temporary situation. How many people have thought similarly and then came to a sudden and abrupt crisis before they died?

We should recall that Lucifer tried the same thing in heaven when he wanted to be like God and refused to live under God's dominion. Hell was created in that instant for Lucifer and the angels who dared to defy God's laws. Here is the humble disposition that you should have when you start your day, which the following prayer demonstrates: *"Jesus, my Lord, my God, my King, my Saviour, my Good Shepherd, my Brother, my Friend, my only Love, my Everything, I open wide the door of my heart to You. I humbly, sincerely, and lovingly invite You to come and dwell within me, to make Your home within me along with the Father and the Holy Spirit for You are all that I desire in the land of the living. I recall Your words and I know they are true: "Behold, I stand at the door and knock. If anyone hears My voice and opens the door, I will come in and dine with him and he with Me." See a heart with a wide open door for You to enter if You so choose."*

7 The Battle for Your Soul

We have just discussed that it takes hard work to be saved and that it is essential to make God the centre of our lives. Let us now look at the challenges we face daily in working out our salvation. We must realize that we are engaged in a battle for our souls. We battle three enemies: the world, the flesh, and the devil. Make no mistake about it, these three enemies are like snipers hiding behind trees as we go about our daily lives. If we leave our homes not thinking that we are in a battle, why would there be any need to put on armor to protect ourselves? So, we trustingly walk out our front door every morning without any armor, that is, without the armor of Christ. We think that we are walking out into the Garden of Eden as we hear the birds singing and see the animals playing. We see the blue skies, we feel the warmth of the sun on our faces, and we feel the gentle breeze. We think how good it is to be alive. And indeed, it is good to be alive.

However, this is no longer the Garden of Eden. Remember, Jesus said, "I saw Satan fall like lightning from heaven" (Lk 10:18). Again, what happened when Satan tempted Jesus in the desert after He had fasted for 40 days? We read: "Again, the devil took Him to a very high mountain and showed Him all the kingdoms of the world and their glory. And he said to Him, "All these I will give You, if You will fall down and worship me"" (Mt 4:8-9). Notice Satan said all the kingdoms of the earth belong to him, and they are his for the giving. Thus, when we walk out into the world every morning, we walk out into a domain that Satan has reconfigured to his plans and designs.

The Garden of Eden was perfect before Adam and Eve sinned. But after Satan tempted them and they sinned, he was given a certain degree of power over the earth to form his type of kingdom. Now, of course, when Jesus came into the world as a man, He ushered in the

The Key, The Door, and The Garden

kingdom of God. From the time of Jesus to now, there has been a battle between Satan's kingdom and the kingdom of God. But make no mistake about it, we are not living in the Garden of Eden before Adam and Eve's fall. We are living on a battlefield where God and Satan are battling for our souls. If you unassumingly do not believe this, either consciously or subconsciously, then, of course, you would not be putting on the armor of Christ when you leave your home. The battlefield awaits you where the world, the flesh, and the devil, the three enemies of your soul, are lurking like hidden snipers. They are sometimes present in the situations and people you meet.

If you do not have on the armor of Christ, you will be easy prey for these three snipers of your soul. And what will be the end of your life? What will it look like if you have not been diligent in defending your soul against these three enemies? It could mean eternal damnation because you were not solicitous with your soul, and you would have allowed these three enemies to conquer you. I warn you, and I encourage you to rise and fight these three enemies. Put on the armor of Christ before you leave your home by trying to spend time in prayer with the Lord.

Our Lady of Medjugorje has said, "I give you the five stones that will slay your Goliath." The five stones are daily Mass, daily Rosary (all four sets of mysteries if possible), monthly Confession, reading Scripture daily, and fasting on bread and water on Wednesdays and Fridays. This is one way of putting on the armor of Christ against the enemy. Why would God allow his Mother to visit the earth every day since 1981? A nun named Sister Emmanuel Maillard went to Medjugorje a long time ago, and was very impressed and touched by what she saw. She really believed in her heart that God was sending our Lady to rescue humanity from its dire state of destruction. Sister Emmanuel made it her life's mission to take other pilgrims to

Medjugorje. On one occasion, she was speaking with a French Bishop about Our Lady of Medjugorje's apparitions. The French Bishop said to her: Sister Emmanuel, I see the good fruits of Medjugorje, but one thing puzzles me about it, and that is, all the other appearances of Our Lady throughout history have lasted just a few months, maybe five or six apparitions to some children within three to six months, and then they were over. What puzzles me about Medjugorje is its excessiveness - Our Lady has been appearing there every day for 20 to 30 years! That puzzles me, and I cannot understand or even believe that God would allow such an excessive phenomenon. He was almost trying to discredit Medjugorje because of the excessiveness of Our Lady's appearances. Then, Sister Emmanuel wisely said to him: Your Excellency, if you had a son who was seriously ill and was in the critical care ward of the hospital, would you visit him every day? He paused, and he said: Sister, I understand what you are saying. She said yes, Medjugorje is the critical care ward of the world.

The patients (you and I) are critically ill. Therefore, God has been allowing His Mother Mary to visit us (the patients) every day since 1981. Do not be astounded by the excessiveness of the Our Lady's appearances in Medjugorje; they are necessary for the world because we, the patients, are critically ill. And why are we so seriously ill? Because we do not understand or even believe that we are in a battle and do not see ourselves as soldiers fighting for the salvation of our souls.

We should also be fighting to help to save the souls of our family members, our friends, our communities, and our countrymen. We have fallen asleep and are walking out of our houses every day into battle without the armor of Christ. We do not have the five stones to slay our Goliath, and we are instead getting slain by Goliath. Thus, we have become like that critically ill patient in the hospital ward, and Our Lady has come to visit us because we are spiritually sick. But make no mistake about it - if we do not listen to Her, and if we do not heed Her messages and put on the armor of Christ by putting those five stones in our pouches, then when we go out to do battle against the Goliath that exists in our lives and the world, we may very well get slain. Goliath exists in your workplace, family, community, and country. Goliaths, in the form of the world, the flesh, and the devil, are everywhere. Remember, Satan said that all the kingdoms of the earth belong to him. If you do not see yourself as David fighting Goliath, you may face eternal damnation at the end of your life. This statement may sound very harsh, but this is a loving message to you from God and His Mother, Mary.

Time is short. You may say, what if Jesus does not return for another 100 or 200 or 1,000 years? That may very well be the case. For with God, 1,000 years is like a day, and one day is like 1,000 years. No one knows the exact return of Jesus Christ to the world. But the average life expectancy is 80 years. If you are currently 40 years old, there are only 40 more years left in your life before you will meet Jesus and must be judged by Him. Is time short for you? Is time short for me? Absolutely. It cannot be much longer than 80 years. I encourage you to wake up and realize that you are in a battle for your soul and that you are a soldier.

Look at the armies of various countries and see how hard they train; just research what the average soldier does every day to keep his body fit and keep his mind sharp. Do they not talk about the enemy and his tactics? They train to be physically fit. They often run 10 miles a day. They do sit-ups and push-ups. They harden themselves just in case they will be facing the enemy that day. That is just for an earthy battle where the stakes are the death of citizens of their country. They are fighting to try to prevent that. In World War II, when the Allied forces fought, Hitler was an evil force in the world. The stakes there were life and death here on earth and liberty from the Nazi ideology. However, regarding the spiritual battle, we are talking about eternal stakes, not just earthly death, or a lack of earthly freedom. We are talking about eternal life or eternal death. There is an infinite difference between the two because one is never-ending sadness and anguish, which is hell. The other one is eternal happiness, joy, and peace in union with God. We are talking about freedom with God versus complete slavery to the devil in the fires of hell.

The spiritual battle is way more important than any earthly battle that a country may face. Soldiers spend so much time preparing their bodies. They are so rigorous in their training and are so astute in their understanding of the enemy that they may potentially have to face. And that is just for an earthly battle. Why are we Christians not twice as diligent as they are in our preparations? Why are we not doing spiritual exercises as they do physical training? Why are we not studying the enemy forces, which are the world, the flesh, and the devil that assail us every day? These are smarter and more insidious than the earthy enemies that our countries face. Therefore, it is more incumbent upon us to be even more diligent than the soldiers in a regular army. The choice is up to us. I can only advise you to be more diligent as I encourage myself every day.

We will sometimes fall if we do not put on the armor of Christ adequately against the world, the flesh, and the devil. We will need to use the Sacrament of Confession, which is like the hospital's healing ward, where a injured soldiers go for care. As much as we put on the armor of Christ and have the five stones that Our Lady encourages us to carry with us, now and again, the enemy will wound us. We must go and get healed. That is why Our Lady recommends monthly Confession or even more frequently. That is the healing hospital for your soul. So, put on the armor of Christ and carry the five stones in your pouch every day.

Be diligent and exercise your spirit through prayer, fasting, arms-giving, and by frequenting the Sacraments. Then you will have a great chance of winning the battle for your soul and spending an eternity of joy and peace with God.

Summary

The Christian faces three enemies of his soul daily: the world, the flesh, and the devil. We are not living in the Garden of Eden before the fall of Adam and Eve. We are living on a battlefield where God and Satan are battling for our souls. If you believe this, then you need to put on the armor of Christ when you leave your home. Our Lady of Medjugorje has said, "I give you the five stones that will slay your Goliath." The five stones are daily Mass, daily Rosary (all four sets of mysteries if possible), monthly Confession, reading Scripture daily, and fasting on bread and water on Wednesdays and Fridays. This is one way of putting on the armor of Christ against the enemy.

The world, the flesh, and the devil are waiting like hidden snipers behind every tree, building, situation, and sometimes even behind some people you meet. If you do not have on the armor of Christ, you will be easy prey for these three snipers of your soul. And what will be the end of your life? You could risk losing your soul for all eternity.

8 Build Your House on Rock and Guard Your Dignity

After discussing the need and urgency to take the salvation of your soul very seriously and putting on the armor of Christ daily, I would like to discuss something more subtle that can happen to every one of us. It involves the gradual loss of our dignity. Do not let anyone take away your dignity because it can happen without you even noticing it. Whitney Houston sang a song, but the song was wrong. In "The Greatest Love," she said the following words: "They can't take away my dignity." But, if you look at her life and how it ended, she did lose her dignity. She allowed those with whom she associated during her years in Hollywood and the music industry to take away her dignity. We have to be careful not to speak proudly like that, not that she intended to. I am sure Whitney Houston had all good intentions when she said: "they can't take away my dignity." But when we look at how Whitney Houston's life ended, and even how her own daughter's life ended, we see that she did lose her dignity.

We notice a similar attitude in the Apostle Peter on the night of Jesus' betrayal. Peter said: "Though they all fall away because of You, I will never fall away" (Mt 26:33). Jesus then said to Peter: "Truly, I tell you, this very night, before the rooster crows, you will deny Me three times" (Mt 26:34). Peter was insistent: "Even if I must die with you, I will not deny You!" And all the disciples said the same" (Mt 26:35). We look at what happened with Peter in the courtyard when Jesus was being tried, and how he denied Jesus three times, even though he had been with Him for three and a half years and saw His miracles.

We must understand that, as much as we might intend not to let people take away our dignity or as much as we want to be faithful to

God, we must believe that we are weak. Indeed, we can have people take away our dignity, or we can deny the Lord as Peter did. Whitney Houston, in her song, The Greatest Love, should have said: "Don't let them take away your dignity," or "I will try not to let them take away my dignity." What Peter should have said to Jesus was, "I pray that I will not deny you. I pray that I will be able to have the strength to die for you."

A reflection on these two individuals, Peter the Apostle and Whitney Houston, the late singer, should make us reflect on our frailty and shortcomings. We all have good intentions. When Jesus asked the Apostles, Peter, James, and John in the garden of Gethsemane to stay awake and pray for one hour with him, they had all intentions to do what He asked of them. When Jesus went away, He knelt in prayer, and during His agony, He even sweated blood. Jesus came back and found them asleep. He did this three times, and every time He came back, they were sleeping. Eventually, He said to them, "Watch and pray that you may not enter into temptation. The spirit indeed is willing, but the flesh is weak" (Mt 26:41).

Our minds might be willing to not let people take away our dignity, and our minds might want to not deny the Lord. However, our flesh is weak, and we can easily deny the Lord. We can easily allow other people to take away our dignity. When our dignity is robbed from us, it usually happens very slowly and sometimes right from under our nose, without us even realizing it.

Some of the greatest tragedies that happen to us human beings happen in slow degrees. Yes, we have drastic things that happen to us, like deaths in our families. But sometimes, when these things happen, they are usually out of our control. But the most sinister things that we must be more on guard for are the ones that occur slowly, where we do not realize that they are happening to us. In the case of Whitney Houston, when she started as a gospel singer, and she sang the words of that song, "They can't take away my dignity," I am sure she did not doubt that anyone could ever take away her dignity as a human being. But we see how her life ended, and we see that in slow degrees, Whitney Houston had her dignity robbed of her, right from under her nose, but in slow degrees.

We must be on guard in our lives, even sometimes within our own families. That is sad to say. It is not that people intentionally want to rob us of our dignity. I doubt that people generally look at us and say, "I will deprive that person of their dignity." I do not think that the people with whom Whitney Houston associated in the music industry set out with an overt plan to rob her of our dignity. But again, we are all fallen human beings, and very often, people are not even aware of the consequences of their actions and words towards others. That is why we must be vigilant.

Jesus warned us when he said, "Stay awake and pray." St. Paul said: "Pray at all times." We must be vigilant because the enemies of our souls are varied, sinister, and very subtle. Each day that we live our lives in this world, we must be on guard. We must be prayerful people not to have our dignities robbed from right under our nose. Remember that it happens in slow degrees. Look at what has occurred with the television, movie, and music industries. In slow degrees from the 1960s onwards, things have slowly degenerated in terms of morality, violence, and all the evil we see today in the media and the world.

You may have heard the story of how to boil a frog. If you put a frog into a pot of hot water, the frog will immediately jump out. However, if you put a frog into a pot of cool water and slowly turn up the temperature, the frog will not notice that the water is getting hotter and hotter. Eventually, the frog will boil to death. Similarly, our dignities can be robbed from us. It happens in slow degrees, with the temperature being turned up slowly and without us noticing it day to day, month to month, year to year. Suddenly, we reach a stage in our lives when we could be like Whitney Houston, where our dignities have been robbed from us, and we now face not just physical death, but possibly spiritual death.

No one can judge where Whitney Houston went or where any other soul may have gone after death. Judas betrayed Jesus for 30 pieces of silver and then hung himself. Jesus said of Judas: "The Son of Man goes to His destiny. But woe to that man by whom He was betrayed. Better for that man if he had not been born" (Mt 26:24). Jesus implied that Judas did not go to a happy place when he died. Theologians St. Augustine and St. Thomas Aquinas have concluded that Judas went to hell. Hence, we must realize that if we are not vigilant, we can even lose our souls. Not only can our dignity be robbed from us, but we may have a situation where we end up in desperation and despair, and we end up without any hope. It would seem to have happened to us overnight. But nothing tragic like that happens overnight. It is due to a long, slow period of degradation of our dignity and the sanctity of our souls.

Jesus calls us to be very vigilant and to watch and pray because we are all responsible for our own lives. If we are not careful, our very existence, souls, and dignity can be robbed from us. So, let us remember that and be very vigilant on a day-to-day basis. When it comes to trusting other people, Jesus Himself gave us a model. In John's gospel, near the end of chapter 2, it is recorded that Jesus was at the festival and had worked many miracles. Scripture tells us: "When they saw all the signs that He performed, many people came to believe in Him, but Jesus, for His part, did not entrust Himself to them. For He knew all men and needed no one to be a witness to man. For He Himself knew what was in man" (Jn 2:23-24).

If you listen to that passage carefully, Jesus loved everyone. But He did not trust anyone because He Himself knew what was in man. Neither you nor I am trustworthy. No one in this world is trustworthy. Only God can be trusted. We may have good intentions towards ourselves and towards other people. But because of our fallen nature, we are not trustworthy.

To love someone else does not mean that you must trust them. You absolutely must be vigilant. You must watch each person's every motive, listen to their every word, and discern what they are saying. Discern their life's principles and what they stand for. That could even mean your parents. It could be your sisters, your brothers, or your friends.

Every single human being has a fallen nature. We are essentially good, but we do carry some evil within us. We must be careful when we listen to what other people tell us, even what they try to teach us. We must filter everyone's words through the Gospel's lens and take what is right and leave what is wrong.

In the Gospel, Jesus again advised us, "If anyone comes to Me and does not hate his own father and mother and wife and children and brothers and sisters, yes, and even his own life, he cannot be My disciple" (Lk 14:26). Now, did Jesus mean that we should literally hate our mother and father, our brothers, and our sisters? No, He was using hyperbole, which is a type of exaggeration. What He meant was, if you come to Me and accept everything that your family tells you, or everything that your friends tell you, without first discerning whether it forms part of My teachings for you, then you cannot be My disciple. If you simply accept it because that person is your

The Key, The Door, and The Garden

mother, or your father, or your friend, or your brother or sister, then you love that person more than you love God.

To honor and to respect your parents does not mean that you should agree with everything they tell you. Your parents are also fallen, and they too are sinful, just like you and me. Whenever your mother or your father tells you something, you must respect them. You do not dishonor them. But at the same time, you must discern whether what they have told you is correct. Is it in line with Jesus' teachings and His values, or is it not? Remember that St. Francis of Assisi disowned his father's wealth when he stripped naked in front of the bishop's tribunal and then proceeded to live a life of poverty in imitation of Jesus, much to his father's chagrin. Most of the people in the town of Assisi thought that he had gone mad because they did not understand that he wanted to radically follow Jesus and the Gospel values that Jesus came to teach us. St. Francis of Assisi became one of the greatest and holiest Saints that the Catholic Church has ever known, as witnessed by the fact that the Franciscan order within the Church currently has over 30,000 friars worldwide and countless third-order members.

When I offered Leadership, Career, and Life Coaching, many young people came to me in a state of tension. I sensed either explicitly or implicitly the amount of pressure that their parents placed on them to pursue a very prestigious career like medicine, law, or engineering. These careers would lead them to have a lot of money one day, a lot of prestige and power in society. Parents who do that to their children do not want to hurt them. They are not trying to deliberately lead their children astray, but they are imposing their values or unfulfilled dreams on their children.

If someone is called to medicine, law, engineering, politics, or business, that is fine. If you are called to that by God, there is nothing wrong with pursuing those professions. But not everyone is called to those professions. Sometimes parents feel that unless their child has a prestigious profession and looks good in society's eyes, then their child is a failure, and they have not done a good job as parents. However, if that child of yours was not destined for that career by God and that is not their purpose or mission in life, then yes, you are leading them astray, not explicitly but implicitly. Your advice to that child is robbing that child of his or her God-given mission or purpose in life, and in a way, you are robbing them of their dignity.

For example, I am sure that when Whitney Houston achieved stardom in the music industry and in Hollywood, she thought she was doing a good thing. She was going from being a gospel singer to becoming a star with lots of money. Who would think on the surface that there was anything wrong with this? Then, she got into drugs and probably other types of substance abuse. Eventually, she lost her very life. I pray that she did not lose her soul.

Do you see how people can have well-meaning intentions but very worldly values? And this is what Jesus calls us to discern. Are we living the Gospel that He preached, or are we living our own gospel or the gospel of the world? Very often, we are living a hybrid gospel. We regularly take Jesus' Gospel, and we combine it with our gospel. This is known as being a cafeteria Christian. We pick and choose what we want, and we combine it with our ingredients. We take some of the advice that Jesus gave in His teachings, and we leave other advice out that we do not like and that do not suit our values. Jesus said: "Brother will deliver brother over to death, and the father his child, and children will rise against parents and have them put to death, and you will be hated by all for My name's sake. But the one who endures to the end will be saved" (Mt 10:21-22).

The Key, The Door, and The Garden

We often look at the Gospel, and we hear some of these things that Jesus said, and they do not make any sense to us. Most of all, they would lead us to a life of suffering and inconvenience, and we would not end up with a good reputation in the eyes of the world, our family, or our community. We then conveniently ignore those challenging words that Jesus said, and we substitute them with our ideologies and values. That is what I mean by living a hybrid gospel.

Jesus said that unless a house is built on rock, it will collapse when the winds and the storms of life come. He said the man who builds his house on sand, when the winds come, and the rains fall and beat upon that house, it will fall. And what a great fall it will have.

Firstly, we can choose to build our house on rock, which is the Gospel of Jesus Christ taught by the Catholic Church. Many other churches claim they have the correct interpretation of the Gospel, but this varies from church to church. At last count, there were over 33,000 non-Catholic Christian denominations in the United States alone.

Jesus Christ has given the Magisterium of the Catholic Church the authority to safeguard the truths of the Gospel. There are many ways to interpret the Gospel, but there is only one Church left by Jesus, with the Apostle Peter being the first pope, i.e., the first head of the Church. We must be careful when we say we are living by the Gospel. Which gospel and whose interpretation of the Gospel? To build our house on rock means that we must try to live our lives based on the Gospel of Jesus Christ as safeguarded by the Catholic Church. That is what it means to build your house on rock.

Secondly, what does it mean to build your house on sand? Essentially, it means to ignore the Gospel of Jesus Christ altogether and live your life on your values or the values of the world.

Build Your House on Rock and Guard Your Dignity

There is a third possibility implied here. We can sometimes build our houses on a combination of rock and sand. That is a combination of Jesus' Gospel and our values, or a combination of Jesus' Gospel and the world's values. That is a hybrid gospel, which leads to a somewhat weak foundation.

The winds will come, the rains will fall, and they will beat upon our houses. Of the three houses, the one built on sand, which has nothing of the Gospel of Jesus and everything of the values of the world or your values and opinions, will be the quickest one to fall. Similarly, the third house, which is built on a combination of rock and sand, which is a combination of Jesus' Gospel and worldly values, will eventually fall too. It will take longer, but ultimately, that house will fall also. The only houses that will remain standing when the tribulations that Jesus spoke about come upon the world, will be those who have built their lives on the rock of Jesus Christ and His Gospel as taught by the Catholic Church. Those are the people whose souls will be left with their dignity intact.

We are at a point in history when many tragedies are happening globally – geopolitically, environmentally, and on a personal level. I have seen many tragedies with my own eyes in families, and many people struggling with health and financial problems. There are the issues of crime in society and much upheaval in the world and within families. These are all signs that God is warning the world both personally and globally, that time is running out.

We each need to look within ourselves to see whether our houses are built on rock, built on sand, or built on a combination of rock and sand. No one can answer that question, but you or I, and we must be honest. We must look at the foundation of our houses, which is the foundation of our souls and our lives. And we must be truthful. Speak to someone who is in construction, for example, a civil engineer or a

The Key, The Door, and The Garden

construction worker. They will tell you that to build a stable house that can withstand any kind of storm or earthquake, you must first excavate the land on which the house will be constructed. You must dig very deep, and you must remove all the dirt, all the debris, and all the rocks and boulders in that lot before you even lay the foundation.

That is an excellent analogy for the spiritual work that we must do in our souls. Do we excavate? Do we remove the dirt and debris within our souls, that is, our sinful tendencies and habits, or even things that exist in our lives because of inherited traditions? We often justify our actions by saying: "My mother and father did this, or my husband did this, or my culture does that, or we've always done it this way. We have always sought after money and big houses, and unbridled profit-driven businesses. It must be right because it's part of our tradition." But we must stop and examine carefully, and we must put everything in our lives under the microscope of Christ and His Gospel. When the engineer, the construction workers, and the foreman get to the lot, they look at the lot and see what boulders there are. They must see what machinery they need to bring to excavate that lot to make sure that it becomes an empty pit. They must remove all debris and obstructions for the lot to be clear when the time comes to pour the concrete. This will lead to a strong foundation.

Firstly, we must each consider our lives and see what areas of sin exist, and not only that, but what traditions we have inherited from our parents, our culture, and our country, and then ask ourselves: "are these of Jesus Christ?" Do they stand up to the Gospel values? And if they do not, we must excavate them, and we must get rid of them. Otherwise, our house will not stand when the trials of life come upon us from time to time, and especially when the Great Tribulation predicted by Jesus in Matthew, chapter 24, comes upon the world. Our houses will not stand. Let us therefore excavate and let us not be selective. Let us remove everything that is not of God from our lives. That is the first step. It takes a brave person to do that, to be willing to fly in the face of society and family traditions, and to excavate, but it must be done.

Secondly, what kind of concrete are we going to pour into the foundation of our houses? Are we going to buy the cheapest concrete and the quickest to one to set? Maybe it is concrete mixed with useless filler, and we will just pour the foundation with that concrete. That again is building on a hybrid gospel, the Gospel of Jesus combined with your values and those of our society or our culture or family. That, too, is not wise. We must pour pure concrete; the gospel of Jesus Christ must be poured into our lives after we excavate all those sins and traditions that are not of God.

Remember again, Jesus said: "If anyone comes to Me and does not hate his own father and mother and wife and children and brothers and sisters, yes, and even his own life, he cannot be My disciple" (Lk 14:26). Jesus is the rock on which our faith is built.

Make sure that we pour pure concrete into the foundation of our houses, of our souls. The foundation, however, takes time to set. That is why time is of the essence. Time is short, and we do not have a lot of time. We cannot build a house overnight, a stable home that will withstand storms and rains and winds. Excavation takes time. Discovering the right concrete takes time and effort, and so does pouring it. Building a solid foundation takes time, and we must allow time for the foundation to set. Once it has set, you can now start building your house on top of the foundation. That takes time. Conversion is not an overnight activity. It takes time; it takes work, blood, sweat, and tears, and most of all, it takes commitment. Not many people are willing to build the house of their soul in such a thorough fashion. But what will be the consequence of not doing so?

The result will be dire. When the tribulations of life come upon us, which we are now seeing in the world around us and in our own families, will our houses stand? Only you and I can answer that question personally.

Summary

I pray that every human being will stop and take stock of their lives and look at their foundation. If they need to rebuild their house, do it quickly because each stage takes time. Excavate, build correctly, and get rid of what is not of God. Pour the pure concrete of the Gospel of Jesus Christ as taught by the Catholic Church into your foundation. Let it set firmly and build upon that. Each day that goes by that you do not do this becomes another wasted day, and the storms of life are indeed already upon us. I pray that God will give us all wisdom to embark upon this most important task. Indeed, it is a battle for our very lives and our eternal destinies.

As we reflect on the way Whitney Houston's life ended, we can easily see that if we do not build our houses properly, then yes, they can take away our dignity. My advice to you is the same advice to myself: let us not allow them to take away our dignity. She sang a song, and that song was wrong. Are you singing a song that is wrong? Only time will tell, and possibly sooner than you think.

9 Emotional, Mental, Physical, and Spiritual Health

Human beings are neither animals nor angels. There are four dimensions or aspects to our being: the emotional, the mental, the physical, and the spiritual. Because of these four areas' connectedness, if we allow one or more of them to become weakened, it can negatively affect the others without us knowing it. I have observed many people during my lifetime who are emotionally wounded from childhood and spend many hours hiding their pain in Churches and chapels. I highly recommend spending a half-hour at Mass daily and, if possible, an hour in a Blessed Sacrament chapel adoring Jesus. However, when emotional pain is being masked by hiding from others, it is time to look at our entire being to see where we might need healing to regain balance. Let us proceed to explore each of these four areas now.

Emotional Health

Emotional health is an area that we can all improve upon. We often carry around emotional baggage from our past, and we bury and forget about hurts that go way back to our childhood. The problem is this: emotions are like internal energy that must find an outlet. If bottled up for too long, the negative consequences to our lives and relationships can be profound. We can start the process of healing by building self-awareness about our strengths and limitations.

Without you even knowing it, a lack of emotional health can sabotage your entire life and rob you of living the life that God intended for you. Carrying around emotional hurts and disabling patterns of behavior can also affect the other areas of our lives, such as our spiritual, mental, and even physical health. I have worked for several years with teenage boys and young men from an orphanage in the Caribbean. On most occasions, when I asked them if they believe in their hearts that God loves them, the overwhelming answer was NO! They have experienced so many emotional hurts in their lives that they cannot fathom a loving God who cares about them and loves them personally. They have difficulty praying, exercising, and even concentrating on their schoolwork. The same pattern applies to adults with whom I have worked in a Leadership, Career, and Life Coaching capacity.

How do you know if you have emotional wounds that have not healed? It is simple to answer: if certain events and people keep coming up in your mind over and over, then you have not dealt with those events and people in a way that has brought real closure. I would highly recommend reading John Schurmann's "Emotional Wound First-Aid Kit," which is available in Kindle format on Amazon. Many years ago, it helped me to deal with unresolved emotional wounds in my own life. Schurmann offers specific step-by-step treatments that are fast, simple, and effective. He defines the causes of emotional wounds and what you can do to repair, heal, and maintain optimal health. Schurmann explains how to:

- Assess the seriousness of an emotional injury.
- Care for your emotional sores and support the healing.
- Let go of the injustice, emotional injury, or pain.
- Forgive the person or event.
- Restore damaged relationships and life dreams.
- Protect and strengthen your emotions.
- Become your best friend, to love, trust, and forgive yourself.

- Deepen and enrich your relationships and feel closer to your loved ones.
- Believe in yourself and become a positive person.[20]

Schurmann shows you in the kit a simple way to diagnose if you have unresolved emotional wounds. If you answer Yes to more than one of the following statements, there is reason to suspect that an emotional wound is present in your life:

- I do not forgive people.
- I hold anger or resentment.
- I often suppress my feelings.
- I have trouble trusting people.
- I choose to keep hurtful events a secret.
- I feel guilt or shame.
- I have trouble sharing my feelings.
- I still grieve the loss after so many years.
- I have never let go of betrayal, loss, or hurt.
- I self-medicate with alcohol, drugs, or work[21]

I strongly advise you not to let your lack of emotional health sabotage your relationship with God and your loved ones any longer. Use the advice in the "Emotional Wound First-Aid Kit" or visit a counseling psychologist to work through these wounds. You will feel

---

[20] John Schurmann, *Emotional Wound First Aid Kit: A Comprehensive Workbook for Healing and Optimal Emotional Health & Wellness* (CreateSpace Independent Publishing Platform, 2016).

[21] Ibid.

a weight lifted off your shoulders, and the joy of living will return as when you were a child.

Mental Health

By mental health, I do not mean what most of society thinks it means. Mental health is often confused with emotional health, as the manifestations of emotional woundedness can show up as problematic conditions of the mind. Some examples are depression, anxiety, addictions, obsessive-compulsive behaviour, and the list goes on.

Mental health means having the ability and the opportunity to use your mental faculties to the fullest and to feel like you are not wasting your potential to think and reason. Some people are stuck in a job that they consider "mindless." After having left the workplace to have children, some women can feel that they are mentally stagnant.

Do you know what one of the most significant contributors to mental stagnation is? The excessive amount of time that people today spend on various technology and social media platforms. When was the last time you curled up in bed or on your living room sofa with a good book that stimulated you mentally, and that you looked forward to reading the next night, and the next night, and so on? I spent 24 years in information technology in Toronto, Canada, so I can safely say that I am qualified to give you some sound advice on how to get your mental health back from the modern-day thief of time, technology. It starts by turning off all your digital platforms by 7 PM every night. Does that sound too drastic? Well, I would not be giving you the advice if I were not observing it myself. I do not watch television, I have no online media subscriptions, I do not go to the movies, and I use social media mainly for business purposes.

What, might you ask, does this advice have to do with your mental and spiritual life? Everything, in my opinion. To connect with God, we have to turn off all distractions to prayer, and our modern world certainly provides many such distractions for us. The Catechism of the Catholic Church states the following: "Science and technology by their very nature require unconditional respect for fundamental moral criteria. They must be at the service of the human person, of his inalienable rights, of his true and integral good, in conformity with the plan and the will of God."[22]. Thus, technology must be at the service of man for it to be healthy. When man is at the service of technology, which is sadly the case for most people today, it will lead to our demise. Satan is very smart in the tactics he uses to distract us from our relationship with God.

The moral of the story on mental health as it relates to your spiritual life is to make sure that you are mentally stimulated by having sufficient time for reading and prayer and that you are not distracted and anxious by being mentally over-stimulated by the excessive use of technology.

Physical Health

Many years ago, a friend of mine in Toronto, Canada, went to a talk given by a well-known exorcist from Rome. Everyone in the audience was eager to hear what his advice would be to ward off evil spirits in their lives. They expected the exorcist to start with advice such as blessing yourself frequently with holy water, wearing your brown scapular and a blessed crucifix, covering yourself with the precious

---

[22] *Catechism of the Catholic Church, Second Edition* (Libreria Editrice Vaticana, 1994, 1997), no. 2294.

blood of Jesus before leaving home, which are all great things to do daily. However, he instead said to ensure that you were physically healthy and getting enough rest and exercise! The audience was understandably stunned. He further explained that Satan could easily get to us when our bodies are physically tired and run down.

Modern-day living with its cars, office jobs, and the pervasiveness of technology devices have left most people sedentary and unhealthy. Add to that the easy availability of fast-food outlets, and it is no wonder that most developed nations have an obesity crisis on their hands. Here again, as with our mental health, we have to grab hold of the reins and not let ourselves become victims of the societies in which we live. Trying to eat healthy foods, getting enough exercise every week (approximately three hours of vigorous walking is sufficient), and getting enough sleep, will do wonders for your spiritual life.

Spiritual Health

Now that we have addressed the need for being emotionally, mentally, and physically healthy, it is easy to see how you can build a solid foundation for a spiritually healthy life. Many people struggle with their spiritual life and their relationship with God and often look for the answers in the spiritual realm. They think that they are not saying the right prayers, not praying enough daily, or have unconfessed sins on their consciences, all of which may be true and need to be addressed. But before we go digging in these areas, it pays to check the three other areas of our lives (emotional, mental, and physical) to see if work needs to be done there.

The reality is that we are holistic human beings, and we often have to work on these four areas of our life simultaneously. A good habit

Emotional, Mental, Physical, and Spiritual Health

is to rate yourself at the end of every week from 1 to 10 in each of these areas. A perfect score is 10/10, and 1/10 is the lowest score. Your current scores might look like this, for example:

- Emotional health: 7/10
- Mental health: 6/10
- Physical health: 5/10
- Spiritual health: 4/10

The above example would lead to an overall average score of 5.5/10, which is not very good. Think of yourself as an airplane flying through the skies of life. When your plane starts getting close to 5/10, it runs the risk of dipping below the radar level where air traffic control (your friends and family) can no longer see you. You can even lose the ability to pray and have a healthy relationship with God.

You are the pilot of your plane and when you notice that you are dropping below 6/10, then start pulling up on the yoke. Start exercising more, reading more, expressing your emotions more explicitly, and praying more. An overall healthy person should be flying their "plane" between 6/10 and 9/10. Let us be realistic: no one is ever at 10/10 overall. That would be heaven. Be careful, however, because if you allow your plane to fly too long below 6/10, you can eventually end up at 2/10 or even 1/10, which is clinical depression. I have seen this happen to many people in the past; it was all because they ignored the warning signs in one or more areas of their lives.

Summary

Human beings are not animals and are also not angels. There are four dimensions or aspects to our being: the emotional, the mental, the physical, and the spiritual. Because of these four areas' connectedness, if we allow one or more of them to become weakened, it can negatively affect the other areas without us knowing it. For example, spending hours in a chapel because one has deep emotional wounds that have never been dealt with can lead to frustration. Perform a sincere analysis of yourself in these four areas, giving yourself a score from 1 to 10 in each area. If there are one or more areas that you score low in, then take action to correct these areas and monitor yourself every week. Imbalance in one or more areas can lead to you not living the healthy life that God intends for you.

PART 2: THE FOUNDATION

If you do not meet God every morning before beginning your day, you will spend the rest of your day looking for Him in those you meet and with whom you interact. You will be left empty and disappointed because no one can take the place of God. *This is one of the most significant causes of broken relationships, idolatry, addictions, and sin in the world.*

"Behold, I stand at the door and knock. If anyone hears My voice and opens the door, I will come in to him and dine with him, and he with Me." (Rev 3:20)

"I wait for the Lord, my soul waits, and in His word, I hope; my soul waits for the Lord more than watchmen for the morning." (Ps 130:5-6)

"Wisdom is radiant and unfading, and she is easily discerned by those who love her and is found by those who seek her. She hastens to make herself known to those who desire her. *He who rises early to seek her will have no difficulty,* for he will find her sitting at his gates." (Wis 6:12-14)

10 The Key

The groundwork for spiritual hunger was laid in the first nine chapters of this book for a reason. Unless you understand the need and urgency of getting your relationship with God on a sure footing and keeping it there, why would you want to discover what The Key is that leads to The Door that opens to The Garden? I will assume that you are sufficiently convinced and motivated to want to discover more about how to develop a better relationship with God, who loves you dearly and wants you to spend eternity with Him in heaven.

In the beginning, when God created Adam and Eve, there was a key, a door, and a garden. The key was this: Adam and Eve were supposed to obey God and not eat of the fruit of the tree of knowledge of good and evil. The door was meant to keep Adam and Eve safe from all outside influences entering and spoiling the paradise that existed there. The garden was, of course, Eden, which was perfect in every sense. In the Book of Genesis, we read:

> When no bush of the field was yet in the land and no small plant of the field had yet sprung up - for the LORD God had not caused it to rain on the land, and there was no man to work the ground, and a mist was going up from the land and was watering the whole face of the ground - then the LORD God formed the man of dust from the ground and breathed into his nostrils the breath of life, and the man became a living creature. And the LORD God planted a garden in Eden, in the east, and there he put the man whom he had formed. And out of the ground the LORD God made to spring up every tree that is pleasant to the sight and good for food. The tree of life was in the midst of the garden, and the tree of the knowledge of good and evil.

The Key, The Door, and The Garden

The LORD God took the man and put him in the garden of Eden to work it and keep it. And the LORD God commanded the man, saying, "You may surely eat of every tree of the garden, but of the tree of the knowledge of good and evil you shall not eat, for in the day that you eat of it you shall surely die."

Then the LORD God said, "It is not good that the man should be alone; I will make him a helper fit for him." Now out of the ground the LORD God had formed every beast of the field and every bird of the heavens and brought them to the man to see what he would call them. And whatever the man called every living creature, that was its name. The man gave names to all livestock and to the birds of the heavens and to every beast of the field. But for Adam there was not found a helper fit for him. So the LORD God caused a deep sleep to fall upon the man, and while he slept took one of his ribs and closed up its place with flesh. And the rib that the LORD God had taken from the man he made into a woman and brought her to the man. (Gen 2:5-9, 15-22)

Alas, we all know that Adam and Eve did not use the key (their obedience to God's command to not eat of a particular tree) to remain in right relationship with God. They were then expelled from the garden of Eden. An angel was placed with a flaming torch to guard the "door" to the garden so that Adam and Eve would not try to enter and eat from the tree of life: "Then the Lord God said, "Behold, the man has become like one of us in knowing good and evil. Now, lest he reach out his hand and take also of the tree of life and eat, and live forever—" therefore the Lord God sent him out from the garden of Eden to work the ground from which he was taken. He drove out the man, and at the east of the garden of Eden he placed the cherubim

The Key

and a flaming sword that turned every way to guard the way to the tree of life" (Gen 3:22-24).

Since the fall of Adam and Eve, the world has been plagued with every kind of suffering, including sin, diseases, toil and frustration in work, pain in childbirth, family problems and marriage breakdowns, wars, pollution, death, and the list goes on. We all feel the frustration that something is not right with the world and with us. We either consciously or subconsciously feel somewhat disconnected from God and one another. When most of us get up in the morning, we are at best cautiously optimistic that we might have a good day, where things may go our way. When they do not go as planned, we are not that surprised because we have grown used to living in a fallen world. Does it have to be this way?

The great Saint and Doctor of the Church, St. Augustine of Hippo, once famously said: "Our hearts were made for Thee O God, and they will never rest until they rest in Thee." If you do not meet God every morning before beginning your day, you will spend the rest of your day looking for Him in those you meet and with whom you interact. You will be left empty and disappointed because no one can take the place of God. This is one of the most significant causes of broken relationships, idolatry, addictions, and sin in the world.

I have now set the stage for explaining "The Key" that forms part of this book's title. This revelation came to me one day when I returned from my pilgrimage to Medjugorje in 2019. I had hoped that this pilgrimage would lead me to instant holiness, especially since I had been following Our Lady's messages for 30 years. I was trying to live a life carrying the "five stones" that Our Lady recommended from the early years of the apparitions (daily Mass, daily Rosary, daily reading of the Bible, monthly Confession, and fasting twice a week on bread and water). Alas, I found myself still struggling to live a holy life and avoiding sin altogether. In exasperation, I cried out to the Lord one day while near the top of a mountain to show me what was missing in my spiritual life because I knew it was something small but significant. That is when I heard a gentle voice say to me:

> *The Key relates to what time you are starting your prayers and spiritual activities for the day. Think of the flower that opens itself up to receive the early morning dew and so is strengthened to endure the heat of the sun during the day, as well as the heavy rains if they come. Compare that to the flower that does not open itself up to the early morning dew; it is wilted even before the day begins and cannot endure the sun and heavy rain. Even if such a soul says many prayers throughout the day, its prayer foundation is missing, and it can easily crumble under the trials and temptations of that day.*

Furthermore, when I came home that day after hearing the Lord's gentle voice speak to me about "The Key" that I was missing in my spiritual life and relationship with Him, I asked the Holy Spirit for a confirmation from Scripture. After praying fervently about this, I randomly opened the Bible, and the following passage was what the Spirit led me to. I would like you to read it in its entirety because the more you read it, the more insight you will gain:

The Key

Song of Songs 5:2-9, 6:1-3

"I slept, but my heart was awake.
A sound! My beloved is knocking.
"Open to me, my sister, my love,
   my dove, my perfect one,
for my head is wet with dew,
   my locks with the drops of the night."
I had put off my garment;
   how could I put it on?
I had bathed my feet;
   how could I soil them?
My beloved put his hand to the latch,
   and my heart was thrilled within me.
I arose to open to my beloved,
   and my hands dripped with myrrh,
my fingers with liquid myrrh,
   on the handles of the bolt.
I opened to my beloved,
   but my beloved had turned and gone.
My soul failed me when he spoke.
I sought him, but found him not;
   I called him, but he gave no answer.
The watchmen found me
   as they went about in the city;
they beat me, they bruised me,
   they took away my veil,
   those watchmen of the walls.
I adjure you, O daughters of Jerusalem,
   if you find my beloved,

The Key, The Door, and The Garden

    that you tell him
        I am sick with love.
What is your beloved more than another beloved,
        O most beautiful among women?
What is your beloved more than another beloved,
        that you thus adjure us?
"Where has your beloved gone,
        O most beautiful among women?
Where has your beloved turned,
        that we may seek him with you?
"My beloved has gone down to his garden
        to the beds of spices,
to graze in the gardens
        and to gather lilies.
I am my beloved's and my beloved is mine;
        he grazes among the lilies." (Song 5:2-9, 6:1-3)

This passage is not the only isolated Scripture passage showing us what The Key is to our relationship with God. I will quote four more Scripture passages to help you see the point the Lord is trying to make to us:

"Behold, I stand at the door and knock. If anyone hears My voice and opens the door, I will come in and dine with him, and he with Me." (Rev 3:20)

"And when He rose from prayer, He came to the disciples and found them sleeping for sorrow, and He said to them, "Why are you sleeping? Rise and pray that you may not enter into temptation." (Lk 22:45-46)

The Key

"I wait for the Lord, my soul waits, and in His word, I hope; my soul waits for the Lord more than watchmen for the morning." (Ps 130:5-6)

"Wisdom is radiant and unfading, and she is easily discerned by those who love her and is found by those who seek her. She hastens to make herself known to those who desire her. *He who rises early to seek her will have no difficulty*, for he will find her sitting at his gates." (Wis 6:12-14)

Let us analyze what is going on with the bride in the Scripture passage from the Song of Songs quoted above. You will notice that the bridegroom (the Lord) comes knocking on the bride's door. There is a clue as to what time He comes knocking: He says, "my head is wet with dew, my locks with the drops of the night." This implies that the bridegroom has come early in the morning before the sun has risen. Here is an important point that God is making to us: He does not like the competition of the busyness and noise that often marks our day when the sun has risen. The cars can already be heard in our streets, your cell phone may have already started to alert you to waiting messages, your children (if you have any) have already begun making demands on your time, and the list goes on. How then can we give God the uninterrupted and quiet time that He deserves and which He so desperately wants to have with each one of us before our day begins? God is a passionate lover, and He does not want you to give Him scraps of your time when you remember to do so. Would you treat your best friend or your spouse that way? I hope not!

Next, notice the attitude of the bride in the above reading from the Song of Songs. She hears her beloved knocking, but she starts to make excuses not to get up and open the door. "I had put off my garment; how could I put it on? I had bathed my feet; how could I soil them?" This attitude sounds all too familiar, and I am sure we can add many more excuses of our own. The main reason modern man does not want to rise early to open the door of his heart to the Lord is that he is tired and needs some extra sleep. Why is this so common? Technology is stimulating and keeping people up too late at night, and by the time most people get to bed, it is near midnight or even after.

Near the end of this book, you can review the results of the author's spiritual survey conducted in May 2020. Here are two interesting findings: 75% of the respondents said that they go to bed after 10:00 PM, and not surprisingly, 65% said that they wake up after 6:00 AM, which is usually after sunrise. We have allowed technology and modern living to sabotage our priorities regarding our relationship with God.

Next, we see that the bride finally gets up to open the door, but alas, she is too late: "I opened to my beloved, but my beloved had turned and gone." This is a very critical verse and one that should sober us up. Why did the beloved turn and leave so quickly? It is because He is a passionate lover and expects us to be the same in return. The bride hesitated because she had found several excuses (all self-serving) not to get up immediately when she heard her beloved knocking at her door. The message she sent to her beloved was this: I love you, but not that much to get up right away and open the door of my heart to you. Put yourself in God's shoes for a moment. He loves you more than you can imagine, and He wants you to spend the first part of your day with Him before all the noise and busyness of the day begins. He wants you to be able to hear His voice when He speaks to you. That is why He comes early in the morning. When you hesitate to get off your bed to spend time with Him in prayer,

The Key

you harm God's relationship with you for the moment, and He turns and leaves. There is hope, though, because your beloved will return early every morning and knock at the door of your heart until the day you die. That is how much God loves you and me and how much He desires to have an intimate and passionately loving relationship with each of us.

The bride now lives with regret for the rest of the day for not opening the door quickly enough to her beloved: "My soul failed me when he spoke. I sought him, but found him not; I called him, but he gave no answer." Worse than that, here is what happens to her next: "The watchmen found me as they went about in the city; they beat me, they bruised me, they took away my veil, those watchmen of the walls." Do you know what this is the equivalent of in our lives? The enemies of our lives will beat us and wound us, and they will take away our protection (our veils) from us, all because we hesitated in rising early and promptly to open to our Lord when He knocked.

We have in our possession many keys that open various doors in lives. Our free will represents the base and stem of each key. The grooves in each key are different because they denote our passions and our heart's desires. A unique and powerful key is the one that opens The Door, who is Jesus Christ, and which leads to The Garden where He pastures His flock among the lilies. The other keys open the doors of the world, the flesh, and the devil, and they can lead to eternal perdition if we do not turn back from them. Many people do not use this unique Key that leads to Jesus Christ, The Door, and sadly have even lost it. Let us find that unique Key and fine-tune its grooves, lubricate it, and use it frequently so that it can open The Door early every morning, who is Jesus Christ, and who fills our days with His graces and who leads us to eternal life.

The Key, The Door, and The Garden

Rising early and giving the first hour or two to the Lord in prayer sets us on the path to keeping the first Commandment of putting God in the first place in your life. Conversely, not rising early to pray, sends a strong message to the Lord that He is not the most important person in your life. Your interests, such as entertainment (which you indulged in the night before and which has caused you not to be able to rise early), are more important to you than waking early to spend time with the Lord. This self-centeredness was the bride's problem in chapter 5 of the Song of Songs, and for the entire day, she paid dearly for not rising early!

Here is a sobering thought: if you do not try to keep the first Commandment, you will have difficulty keeping the other nine Commandments because the first Commandment forms the foundation for all the other nine. Secondly, if you are not consistently keeping the Ten Commandments, how can you proceed to the next level of holiness that Jesus calls us to, and that is, trying to live the Beatitudes? In his encyclical letter "Veritatis Splendor," St. John Paul II said that all Christians should be keeping the Ten Commandments at a minimum.

We often spend most of our Christian lives looking through the keyhole of our door at Jesus' garden, where He pastures His special flock. We then wonder why we cannot leave our somewhat dark room and be a part of that special flock. This is because we do not know what The Key is, or if we know, we are often too lazy to use it daily. However, if we use The Key daily, we move out of the darkness or semi-darkness that often plagues our lives as Christians and into the light of Jesus' garden.

Suppose someone told you that the president of your country or the pope was coming tomorrow to your house at 3:00 AM to spend time with you. Wouldn't you be excited and go to bed early the night before so that you would be able to rise early the next morning and be ready to open the door of your house when he knocks? Well, every morning, without fail, someone way more important than the president or the pope comes knocking at the door of your heart!

We are all familiar with the phrases: "Early to bed, early to rise, makes a man healthy, wealthy and wise," and "The early bird catches the worm." There is great wisdom in those two well-known but often forgotten phrases. Do not let the birds put you to shame by starting to praise their Creator before you do. Turn off all distractions: the television, your computer, your cell phone, and go to bed early so that you can rise early to welcome your special guest, Jesus Christ, into your home and your heart.

An essential aid that you should also use to rise early in the morning is to ask your guardian angel to help you have a restful night's sleep and to get you off your bed when your alarm rings, preferably just before 3:00 AM. God has given each of us a guardian angel, and we so underutilize them that I sometimes think they get bored of having very little to do. Here is a simple prayer that you can say to your guardian angel just before you go to bed: "My dear guardian angel, I thank you for all the help that you have given me throughout my entire life. May God reward you for your faithfulness to me. I humbly ask you to help me to get a good night's sleep and to rise early in the morning refreshed and ready to open to door of my heart to my Lord and Saviour Jesus Christ. He deserves the first place in my day, the first place in my life, and the first place in my heart. I thank you in advance for your help. Amen."

3:00 AM is the hour of power in prayer because it is when we can neutralize the devil's efforts and his angels who come to start working covertly to weaken our souls before the day begins. They are like the fifth column within our "city," which seeks to weaken us and destroy our souls from within. That is why we read in Scripture: "And rising very early in the morning, while it was still dark, He departed and went out to a desolate place, and there He prayed" (Mk 1:35). Jesus never lost a single battle with the world, the flesh, and the devil, and He won the entire war when He allowed Himself to be crucified without ever committing a single sin, even forgiving His enemies while they were in the process of torturing Him!

Remember, God cannot be outdone in charity. "But seek first the kingdom of God and his righteousness, and all these things will be added to you" (Mt 6:33). By giving God the first place in your day, you are saying to Him that He is the most important person in your life, and He will respond by leading you to the next step, The Door.

The Motivation for Using The Key Daily

What will provide you with the motivation to rise early every morning of the week (including Saturdays and Sundays)? It was discussed in the chapter entitled "God Loves You Personally – Believe it and Live it." This knowledge of God's love for you personally will provide you with the motivation to rise very early every morning to greet Our Lord as He knocks at the door of your heart and to welcome Him every time with enthusiasm.

An analogy always helps us to understand a concept better. Let us think about a woman who is engaged to the man of her dreams, and their wedding day is fast approaching. I am referring to the old-fashioned type of courtship where the couple practices chastity in all its beauty before marriage. There is excitement, and there is anticipation between this woman and her fiancée. He promises to visit her early every morning before going to work for them to get to know each on another better before their wedding day. Think of how the bride-to-be would prepare herself every night and what condition she would like herself to be found in when her fiancée arrives every morning. She would most certainly ensure that she turns off all distractions the night before and that she gets a good night's rest. She would want to rise very early, probably at least half an hour before her fiancée knocks at the door of her home. She would freshen up and dress decently for her fiancée, and when he knocks, she would welcome him with a warm smile and heart-felt hospitality. Well, I dare say that every morning, something greater than this is offered to every human being on the face of the earth. Our Lord Jesus Christ, the divine Bridegroom, comes early to visit us with a gentle knock at the door of our hearts. What is sad is that most people do not respond to His call to a loving relationship. This stems from the fact that most people do not believe in their hearts that God loves them personally. If they did, and if they believed the words of Scripture quoted in this chapter, then many more people would rise early every morning without fail to welcome the most passionate Lover in the universe.

Use These Three Small Keys Throughout The Day

The Christian journey through this life is a difficult one, and is full of challenges and surprises. Using The Key that we just discussed in this chapter is the equivalent of opening the main door of your spiritual house early to allow the Lord to enter. Your spiritual house has other doors and windows that the enemies of your soul may try to enter as your day progresses. I would strongly recommend using one or more of the following three small "keys" frequently throughout the day, especially when you feel the first signs of temptation alighting upon you (i.e., the peace within your heart starts to get disturbed).

The Key, The Door, and The Garden

The first small key is a prayer of invitation to the Lord that was mentioned in chapter 6 of this book: *"Jesus, my Lord, my God, my King, my Saviour, my Good Shepherd, my Brother, my Friend, my only Love, my Everything, I open wide the door of my heart to You. I humbly, sincerely, and lovingly invite You to come and dwell within me, to make Your home within me along with the Father and the Holy Spirit for You are all that I desire in the land of the living. I recall Your words and I know they are true: "Behold, I stand at the door and knock. If anyone hears My voice and opens the door, I will come in and dine with him and he with Me." See, a heart with a wide open door for You to enter if You so choose."*

The second small key is the following invocation: **"O God come to my assistance. O Lord, make haste to help me,"** which is the first verse of Psalm 70. When said with your whole being to God, you have the guarantee that He will immediately come to assist you in your temptation and moment of need. This is the same invocation that the Church uses six times a day in the praying of the Liturgy of the Hours. The early desert monks walked about all day reciting this first verse of Psalm 70. Here is a small section of what John Cassian (ca. 360 – 435) says about this verse:

> And so for keeping up continual recollection of God this pious formula is to be ever set before you. "O God, come to my assistance; O Lord, make haste to help me," for this verse has not unreasonably been picked out from the whole of Scripture for this purpose. For it embraces all the feelings which can be implanted in human nature, and can be fitly and satisfactorily adapted to every condition, and all assaults.[23]

---

[23] John Cassian, *Conferences, X*

The Key

The third small key is the following prayer: "**Jesus, I trust in You,**" which is the prayer that Jesus told St. Faustina to have inscribed under the image of the Divine Mercy. If you can learn to say this prayer in rhythm with your breathing, it is very powerful and can be used as a means of meditation. When you find your mind assailed by temptation or anxiety, pause, and breathe deeply in and out while saying this prayer. Breathe in deeply and say "Jesus," and then breathe out and say, "I Trust in You." Repeat this prayer exercise until peace returns to your mind and heart. Here are some entries from St. Faustina's Diary about this invocation:

> In the evening, when I was in my cell I saw he Lord Jesus clothed in a white garment. One hand was raised in the gesture of blessing, the other was touching the garment at the breast. From beneath the garment, slightly drawn aside at the breast, there were emanating two large rays, one red, the other pale (...) After a while, Jesus said to me: 'Paint an image according to the pattern you see: with the signature: Jesus, I trust in You'. I desire that this image be venerated, first in your chapel and [then] throughout the world.[24]

> The graces of My mercy are drawn by means of one vessel only, and that is — trust. The more a soul trusts, the more it will receive. Souls that trust boundlessly are a great comfort to Me, because I pour all the treasures of My graces into them. I rejoice that they ask for much, because it is My desire to give much, very much. On

---

[24] St. Maria Faustina Kowalska, Diary of Saint Maria Faustina Kowalska: Divine Mercy in My Soul (Marian Press - Association of Marian Helpers, 1981), 47

the other hand, I am sad when souls ask for little, when they narrow their hearts.[25]

Jesus Rose from the Dead Early on Easter Sunday

Here is yet another reason why rising early in the morning is so important in our spiritual life. Jesus rose from the dead early on Easter Sunday, while it was still dark. We know from Scripture that the women who went to the tomb got there quite early before dawn: "Now on the first day of the week, Mary Magdalene came to the tomb early, while it was still dark, and saw that the stone had been taken away from the tomb" (Jn 20:2). We know from the other Gospel accounts of Jesus' resurrection that while the other women left, Mary Magdalene stayed back weeping because she had not seen her Lord, but only the empty tomb. Due to her perseverance, she was rewarded with a vision of Jesus in His risen state and was given the mission to announce His resurrection to His disciples. What a beautiful reward and responsibility she was given. This is precisely what happens to us when we rise early every morning before dawn while it is still dark and persevere in searching for Jesus. He will "show" Himself to us in many ways and will entrust us with various missions to announce His good news to our friends, family members, and all we meet that day.

Before closing this chapter, let us address a few issues related to The Key. The first issue is that many people will claim that they are "night owls." I have heard this so often, yet I sincerely believe that our biological clocks can be reprogrammed to transition from being night owls to early birds. I have personally done this a few times in my life.

---

[25] Ibid, 1578

The Key

I used to go to bed after 11:00 PM, whereas I now go to bed between 7:00 and 8:00 PM. To switch from being a night owl to an early bird will take time. According to Bill Fish, a certified sleep coach, "it is best to adjust the time you go to bed, and the time you wake up by only 15 minutes per night. It allows your body to become accustomed to the change gradually. You should ease the transition while you shift your body's circadian clock. Your body might not be happy about the change, and you might feel sleepy while you are in transition." Dr. Lynelle Schneeberg, a licensed Clinical Psychologist and Assistant Clinical Professor at Yale School of Medicine, has also provided some ideas on easing the transition.

The second issue we need to address about The Key discussed in this chapter is those who work varying shifts in their jobs and do not have regular 8:00 AM to 4:00 PM jobs. The same principle applies to them since all they need to do is make sure that after they get their seven to eight hours of sleep, they wake up and give the Lord the first place in their lives.

The third issue deals with those who take care of young children or elderly parents at home. Pray and ask the Lord for the grace of divine time and let Him know that you want to rise early to spend the first part of your day with Him in prayer. Try to get your children and spouse to bed early enough by explaining the importance of your relationship and theirs with the Lord. Let everyone get in the habit of turning off all electronic devices by 8:00 PM and getting to bed early enough to rise early. Can you imagine an entire family that goes to bed early and gets up early to give the Lord the first part of their day?

I would like to leave you with one last thought discussed in this chapter on The Key. Every single religious order within the Catholic Church encourages its members to rise early and start their day with prayer. This practice comes from the original rules laid down for monastic life by St. Benedict in the sixth century, who required his monks to rise at 2:00 AM to prayer the vigil component of the Liturgy of the Hours called Matins. The point is that if members of all religious orders find it necessary to rise early before dawn to start their day in prayer, then laypeople like us should take a page out of their book if we too want to grow in and maintain our holiness.

Summary

Rising early in the morning to give the Lord the first place in your day, in your heart, and in your life is The Key to growth in holiness. Turn off all digital distractions early the night before, and know in your heart that the Lord, the King of the universe, will be knocking at your door early the next morning because He does not like competition from the noise of your busy day. An essential aid that you should also use to rise early in the morning is to ask your guardian angel to help you have a restful night's sleep and to help you get off your bed when your alarm rings at the time you set it – preferably just before 3:00 AM.

Remember what the Lord spoke to my heart on the mountain top when I asked Him what I was missing in my spiritual life. It is worth repeating at the close of this chapter:

> *The Key relates to what time you are starting your prayers and spiritual activities for the day. Think of the flower that opens itself up to receive the early morning dew and so is strengthened to endure the heat of the sun during the day, as well as the heavy rains if they come. Compare that to the flower that does not open itself to the early morning dew; it is wilted even before the day begins and cannot endure the sun and*

The Key

heavy rain. Even if such a soul says many prayers throughout the day, its prayer foundation is missing, and it can easily crumble under the trials and temptations of that day.

You should also try using one or more of the following three small "keys" frequently throughout the day, especially when you feel the first signs of temptation alighting upon you (i.e., the peace within your heart starts to get disturbed).

The first small key is a prayer of invitation to the Lord that was mentioned in chapter 6 of this book: *"Jesus, my Lord, my God, my King, my Saviour, my Good Shepherd, my Brother, my Friend, my only Love, my Everything, I open wide the door of my heart to You. I humbly, sincerely, and lovingly invite You to come and dwell within me, to make Your home within me along with the Father and the Holy Spirit for You are all that I desire in the land of the living. I recall Your words and I know they are true: "Behold, I stand at the door and knock. If anyone hears My voice and opens the door, I will come in and dine with him and he with Me." See, a heart with a wide open door for You to enter if You so choose."*

The second small key is the following invocation: **"O God come to my assistance. O Lord, make haste to help me,"** which is the first verse of Psalm 70.

The third small key is the following prayer: **"Jesus, I trust in You,"** which is the prayer that Jesus told St. Faustina to have inscribed under the image of the Divine Mercy.

11 The Door

We have explored what The Key is to our relationship with God. What is The Door opened by The Key? Well, every door has two sides to it with a handle and keyhole. However, this particular door has those components only on the inside because God respects our free will when He knocks. He will not force His way into our hearts. We must use The Key to open The Door from the inside. In other words, we must love God enough to hear His gentle knock and respond immediately by opening the door of our hearts. Any hesitation on our part sends a message to Jesus that we are only half-hearted in our love for Him while His heart burns with love for us. That is why in the passage from the Songs of Songs quoted in the previous chapter, the beloved turned away and left when the bride hesitated in opening the door to Him.

We can say that one side of The Door represents our heart and all that it contains, good and bad. Of course, as we discussed in the previous chapter, The Key to our side of The Door is our rising early to welcome the Lord when He knocks. The other side of The Door represents the heart of Jesus and all of the goodness and love it contains for us. Jesus has told us plainly:

> I am the door. If anyone enters by me, he will be saved and will go in and out and find pasture. The thief comes only to steal and kill and destroy. I came that they may have life and have it abundantly. I am the good shepherd. The good shepherd lays down His life for the sheep. He who is a hired hand and not a shepherd, who does not own the sheep, sees the wolf coming and leaves the sheep and flees, and the wolf snatches them and scatters them. He flees because he is a hired hand and cares nothing for the sheep. I am

The Key, The Door, and The Garden

the good shepherd. I know My own and My own know Me, just as the Father knows Me and I know the Father; and I lay down My life for the sheep. And I have other sheep that are not of this fold. I must bring them also, and they will listen to My voice. So there will be one flock, one shepherd (Jn 10:9-16).

Let us delve deeper into the above Scripture passage and compare it to the passage from the Song of Songs because there are some striking parallels. Firstly, Jesus tells us: "I am the door. If anyone enters by me, he will be saved and will go in and out and find pasture." That is such a comforting message because we all want to be saved from the many trials and temptations that plague our lives. Secondly, a pasture is a place of refreshment and nourishment, and while there is a promise of our physical sustenance here, there is also a spiritual promise in that we will find what we need to feed on to keep our souls healthy. Remember the verse from the Song of Songs: "My beloved has gone down to his garden to the beds of spices, to graze in the gardens and to gather lilies." You and I have to strive to be one of those lilies because a lily represents purity. What can be purer than to give your heart completely to Jesus in a loving, sincere, and always responsive manner? This is precisely what all the Saints did, and it is what you and I are called to strive for.

Next, Jesus tells us that "The thief comes only to steal and kill and destroy. I came that they may have life and have it abundantly." Many people have been lured by the ways of this world and all of its empty promises and have been left wanting or, even worse, broken-hearted and discouraged about life. I am sure that you and I can write books about the hurts and disappointments that we have experienced by trusting anyone or anything but God. Psalm 146 reminds us: "Put not your trust in princes, in a son of man, in whom there is no salvation.

The Door

When his breath departs, he returns to the earth; on that very day his plans perish" (Ps 146:3-4). Jesus promises us that if we put our trust in Him, we will have life and have it abundantly.

Jesus then goes on to say: "I am the good shepherd. The good shepherd lays down his life for the sheep." Ask yourself one question: do you know anyone in your life right now who would be willing to lay down their life for you? You would be hard-pressed to find someone. Jesus willingly laid down His life for you and me and every single person who has ever lived and who will ever live. "For one will scarcely die for a righteous person—though perhaps for a good person one would dare even to die—but God shows His love for us in that while we were still sinners, Christ died for us" (Rom 5:7-8). Not only did Jesus die for everyone in the world, but His death was excruciating and shameful. Imagine being nailed naked to a cross after being scourged and crowned with thorns. He was left to suffocate until He drew His last breath, all while being taunted by the onlookers! He did this out of love for us; many of the Saints regularly gazed upon the crucifix and meditated upon Jesus' passion and death for them personally. There is no more excellent way to inflame your heart with love for Jesus than by actually understanding and appreciating all that Jesus suffered for you.

Here is another famous and beautiful Scripture passage that refers to The Door: "Behold, I stand at the door and knock. If anyone hears My voice and opens the door, I will come in to him and dine with him, and he with Me" (Rev 3:20). If you search online for the above Scripture passage and look at images that artists have created based on it, many of them will not have a handle on the outside of the door where Jesus is knocking. The handle exists only on the inside of the door. This is very significant because, although Jesus is the Son of God and has the power to break down the door to our hearts, He does not because He respects the most fundamental gift given to us when we were created, and that is, our free will.

Let us explore some of the reasons that cause us to keep the door of our hearts closed to Jesus when He knocks. Firstly, most of us have probably suffered a broken heart at some point in our past. Whether it was a breakup in a relationship when we were teenagers or betrayal from one or more friends or colleagues at work, we have all suffered significant disappointments in our relationships with others. We can all safely say that we have been let down many times by broken promises from our elected governments. Here is a common hurtful experience we may have had in our childhood: disappointment from our parents and what they may have inadvertently done to cause us emotional scaring in our adult years.

All these hurts can lead us to become closed-hearted, which, in turn, translates to us mistrusting others and even God. We may find it hard to believe that God knocks at the door of our heart every morning, seeking a personal and intimate relationship with us. After all, is God not merely a much grander version of those we have interacted with during our lives, especially our parents? That is where we make a fundamental and costly mistake, one that Satan is all too happy to see us make. Scripture gives us the way out of this deadly error: "For as the heavens are higher than the earth, so are my ways higher than your ways and my thoughts than your thoughts" (Isa 55:9). We can and must believe that God is infinitely more perfect and loving than anyone we have ever met in our lives. Simply gaze at a crucifix and repeat to yourself that He did that just for you. If you were the only sinner that ever lived, He would have died on the cross out of love for you and to save you from your sins so that you could enjoy an eternity of joy and peace with Him in heaven.

The Door

The second reason for us not wanting to open the door of our hearts to Jesus is that we have become hard-hearted. This is equivalent to the door to a room expanding over time and becoming jammed against the doorframe. This is the opposite of the first reason where we have a wounded heart and do not trust anyone, not even God. When a person has become hard-hearted or perhaps has always been that way, that is a sign of pride, self-reliance, and contempt for the world and even for God.

In "The Seven Capital Sins" by the Benedictine Sisters of Perpetual Adoration, we read about the various forms of pride. It will take time and work to root out your forms of pride, but it will lead you to a more open and humble relationship with God:

> There is a particular kind of pride in each individual, at least a particular kind dominates, though there may be several of its viruses in the same character. This pride determines our temperament or our type of character, or at least is intimately related to it. Searching into our type of pride is very important for obtaining a true knowledge of ourselves, and for making fruitful efforts to root out sin and vice from our life.
>
> If we are of a sanguine temperament, our pride takes the form of self-centeredness. We fall into vainglory.
>
> If we have a choleric temperament, our pride is manifested in a strong self-will.
>
> If we are melancholic, our pride conceals itself under the garb of self-pity and oversensitivity.
>
> If we have a phlegmatic character, our pride inclines us to self-complacency and vanity.
>
> Pride of superiority makes us want to control the lives of others, to impose ourselves on them, to "domineer" over them.

Closely connected with this kind of pride—or perhaps we should say another name for it—is the pride of independence.

The pride of ambition leads us to seek positions or offices of honor and dignity by which we prefer ourselves to others, however worthy they may be.

We may have a pride of spiritual vanity, imagining ourselves to be perfect and our acts always virtuous or finding a thousand reasons to diminish their gravity or excuse our faults when we do acknowledge them.

It may dress itself in the guise of pride of naturalism, in which case we practice no restraint in our behavior, no modesty in our language, no respect in our obedience.

Pharisaical pride leads us to boastfulness and to criticism of others.

Closely linked to this form of pride is the pride of timidity, which stems from unreasonable fear.

The pride of scrupulosity fixes our attention on wrong things, so that we pay exclusive attention to what does not merit such attention, while we are unscrupulous in things which ought to concern us.

Our pride may be centered on our wealth and prosperity, our station in life, our fine clothes, our wit, beauty or strength.

Pride can ruin all the virtues and draw us into all kinds of disorders. The proud person is capable of any sin. "Pride goes before destruction; and the spirit is lifted up before a fall" (Prov. 16:18).[26]

---

[26] Benedictine Sisters of Perpetual Adoration, *The Seven Capital Sins* (Tan Books & Publishers, 2007).

The third reason for us not wanting to open the door of our hearts to Jesus is fear. We are afraid of what a relationship with Jesus will cost us, what He will ask us to give up, and what He will ask us to do for Him. Make no mistake about it; a genuine relationship with Jesus is demanding and certainly involves a lesser or greater degree of suffering depending on the capacity to endure that God has placed in each of us. But we do not have to fear this aspect of our relationship with Jesus because He will give us the strength to endure whatever is God's will for us. Also, when you have offered up your life's suffering to God in union with Jesus' suffering on the cross, you will be rewarded for all eternity with a crown of glory.

Summary

One side of The Door represents our heart and all that it contains, good and bad. As we discussed in the previous chapter, The Key to our side of The Door is rising early to welcome the Lord when He knocks. The other side of The Door represents the heart of Jesus and all of the goodness and love it contains for us.

The door of our heart can be closed because it has been hurt in the past, or because it has become hardened due to pride, or because of fear of the unknown with Jesus. We must try our best to receive emotional healing in the first case (even by seeking professional counseling). Secondly, we must try to practice the virtue of humility, which is the opposite of pride. Thirdly, we must learn to trust Jesus and not be afraid of Him – after all, He only wants the best for us. Then, we will be more likely to open our hearts when Jesus knocks. With our hearts open to Him, we can then enter The Door, which is Jesus' heart full of love, healing, and blessings, and most of all, a heart that desires us to spend eternity with Him in heaven.

12 The Garden

Now that we know what The Key is and what makes up The Door in forging and maintaining a loving relationship with God, let us explore what The Garden is. In the passage from the Song of Songs that was quoted in the chapter "The Key," we see the bride desperately seeking her beloved and asking the other women to help her to find him: "Where has your beloved gone, O most beautiful among women? Where has your beloved turned, that we may seek him with you?" The bride then tells them where her beloved has gone: "My beloved has gone down to his garden to the beds of spices, to graze in the gardens and to gather lilies. I am my beloved's and my beloved is mine; he grazes among the lilies" (Song 6:1-3). There are many powerful images in these few verses, and we need to explore them to see what they mean for us.

The beloved is in his garden, which contains beds of spices and lilies. There are at least 80 types of spices in the world, all of which add flavor to foods, and many of them have good health benefits. Lilies are flowers that represent purity and rebirth. It is quite amazing to observe that the beloved (Jesus) spends His day among the lilies, representing the pure souls who opened the door of their hearts to Him early when He knocked, and they now have His protection and wisdom to guide them throughout the day. Secondly, The Garden where the Lord and His beloved souls are grazing offers aromatic and healthy spices to all who come to visit The Garden. You will find in your life that if you use The Key to open The Door when the Lord knocks, then you will be led to His Garden and be among the lilies, which are other pure souls like yourself who have opened the door of their hearts to Jesus without hesitation. The Garden that Jesus leads you to has all kinds of exciting and healthy benefits. Indeed, you will be able to offer those around you (friends, family members, and co-workers) the "spices" they need for their lives. It could be the right words of encouragement when they are feeling down. It could be giving them fraternal correction when they are doing something harmful to themselves; it could be sound and Godly advice to help them discern the right direction to take in their lives, and the list goes on.

In Matthew's Gospel, Jesus tells us: "You are the salt of the earth, but if salt has lost its taste, how shall its saltiness be restored? It is no longer good for anything except to be thrown out and trampled under people's feet" (Mt 5:13). Thus, it is vitally essential for our lives to be seen by God as not lacking in spices and salt. We would be wasting the time and talents that He has given us, which are supposed to be used for His greater glory and the good and salvation of our fellowman.

Here are some of the blessings that Jesus will provide you with in His Garden. Note that this list is by no means meant to be exhaustive:

Spiritual Blessings

The first type of blessings that Jesus will give you are spiritual ones. There are those we can see and experience in our lives, and there are, of course, hidden ones that we will only realize when we reach heaven:

- The Holy Bible, containing all of the words that God wants man to know and live by in order to be saved.

- Membership and fellowship in His Church, the Catholic Church, which He promised the gates of hell would not prevail against.

The Garden

- Countless faithful priests, bishops, and the pope who guide and minister in His Church.

- Access to the seven Sacraments of the Church, especially the Eucharist and Confession.

- Your very own guardian angel to protect and guide you throughout your earthly journey.

- Access to His Mother Mary who will keep you in the crossing of Her arms as She said to Juan Diego when She appeared to him in Guadeloupe, Mexico in 1531.

- The writings of the Saints to help you on your journey.

- His unconditional mercy for the sins that you commit on a daily basis, as long as you fear God and ask for His forgiveness.

- Various religious orders and movements within the Church with particular charisms and rules of conduct to help you live a holier life in fellowship with like-minded Christians.

- Talented and inspired artists and musicians who help us lift our minds and hearts to God in prayer.

Temporal Blessings

The second type of blessings that Jesus will give you are temporal ones. These we can clearly see in our lives, and they come and go depending on many factors, such as what country and community we live in, our family situation, and work environment:

- Your daily bread as in the Lord's prayer. As theologians have pointed out, this means so many things, but it certainly includes the physical sustenance you need to live on.

- Signs of His presence in nature all around you: the sky, the sun, the clouds, the rain, the stars, the grass, the animals of nature, the mountains, the seas, fruits, vegetables, nuts, grains, and the list goes on.

- The house where you live, your family, your friends, your neighbours, other human beings you can interact with who have been created just like you, in the image and likeness of God.

- Means of transportation to get you to and from work, school, and other places where you need to go.

- The freedom to practice your faith. Even if the country you live in does not afford you that privilege, you can still practice it in the privacy of your home.

- Other blessings particular to your situation.

The Garden

Trials, Hardships, and Temptations

Finally, Jesus' Garden is full of other surprises and quiet areas for you to grow in your spiritual life. After all, if His Garden were predictable and narrow in scope, we would quickly become bored with it. I guarantee you that the longer you spend in His Garden, the more you will discover and be surprised.

As much as I would like to tell you that all the surprises in His Garden are pleasant ones, sometimes they are heartbreaking. He will call you to become conformed to Him - remember that He was the suffering Messiah prophesied in Isaiah, chapter 53. There is another type of "spice" that Jesus will offer you in His Garden, and that is a type of innocent suffering so that you can participate with Him in His saving mission for the world. He does not force this type of suffering on us but gently asks us if we would be willing to help Him save souls. St. John Eudes gives us great insight into the meaning and purpose of suffering:

> We must strive to follow and fulfill in ourselves the various stages of Christ's plan as well as his mysteries, and frequently beg him to bring them to completion in us and in the whole Church. For the mysteries of Jesus are not yet completely perfected and fulfilled. They are complete, indeed, in the person of Jesus, but not in us, who are his members, nor in the Church, which is his mystical body. The Son of God wills to give us a share in his mysteries and somehow to extend them to us. He wills to continue them in us and in his universal Church. This is brought about first through the graces he has resolved to impart to us and then through the works he wishes to accomplish in us through these mysteries. This is his plan for fulfilling his mysteries in us.

The Key, The Door, and The Garden

For this reason, Saint Paul says that Christ is being brought to fulfillment in his Church and that all of us contribute to this fulfillment, and thus he achieves the fullness of life, that is, the mystical stature that he has in his mystical body, which will reach completion only on judgment day. In another place Paul says: I complete in my own flesh what is lacking in the sufferings of Christ.

This is the plan by which the Son of God completes and fulfills in us all the various stages and mysteries. He desires us to perfect the mystery of his incarnation and birth by forming himself in us and being reborn in our souls through the blessed sacraments of baptism and the Eucharist. He fulfills his hidden life in us, hidden with him in God. He intends to perfect the mysteries of his passion, death and resurrection, by causing us to suffer, die and rise again with him and in him. Finally, he wishes to fulfill in us the state of his glorious and immortal life, when he will cause us to live a glorious, eternal life with him and in him in heaven.

In the same way he would complete and fulfill in us and in his Church his other stages and mysteries. He wants to give us a share in them and to accomplish and continue them in us. So it is that the mysteries of Christ will not be completed until the end of time, because he has arranged that the completion of his mysteries in us and in the Church will only be achieved at the end of time.[27]

---

[27] Saint John Eudes, *The mystery of Christ in us and in the Church, From a treatise On the Kingdom of Jesus* (Pars 3, 4: Opera omnia 1, 310-312).

The Garden

Your Special Mission Daily

Jesus always has a special mission for each of His beloved souls who form part of His flock in The Garden. He instructs and nourishes them and then personally accompanies each of them daily on their respective missions for that day. Jesus can simultaneously accompany each of them because He is God and can give them all His undivided attention, even though their respective missions are different. He then brings them back to The Garden to provide them with rest and renewed strength to prepare for the next day's mission.

Summary

The Garden consists of God's blessings when you use The Key that opens The Door, leading you to The Garden. These blessings take three forms: (1) spiritual blessings, (2) temporal blessings, and (3) trials, hardships, and temptations. Jesus spends his day among the lilies in The Garden, which represents the pure souls who have opened the door to their hearts to Him early when He knocked, and they have His protection and wisdom to guide them throughout the day. The Garden where the Lord and his beloved souls are grazing also offers aromatic and healthy spices to all who visit The Garden.

Make use of The Key, The Door, and The Garden every day without fail, and do not let the enemy find you with your guard down. You will then be ready to face your day with peace, joy, and strength, and you will not be trying to make anyone or anything your god. Most of all, an eternity with God in heaven will await you.

PART 3: THE RESPONSE

"Come to Me all you who are weary and who are heavy laden, and I will give you rest. Take My yoke upon you and learn from Me, for I am gentle and humble of heart, and you will find rest for your souls. For My yoke is easy and My burden is light." (Mt 11:28-30)

"Now I rejoice in my sufferings for your sake, and in my flesh, I am filling up what is lacking in Christ's afflictions for the sake of His body, that is, the church." (Col 1:24)

"Truly, truly, I say to you, unless you eat the flesh of the Son of Man and drink his blood, you have no life in you. Whoever feeds on My flesh and drinks My blood has eternal life, and I will raise him up on the last day. For My flesh is true food, and My blood is true drink. Whoever feeds on My flesh and drinks My blood abides in Me, and I in him. (Jn 6:53-56)

"Therefore, let anyone who thinks that he stands take heed lest he fall." (1 Cor 10:12)

13 How to Stop Worrying for the Rest of Your Life

Now that you have learned more about The Key, The Door, and The Garden, God desires a response from you. He wants you to be ready to apply them to your own life. I will provide you with some practical advice and tips in the remaining chapters of this book to help you apply what you have learned and make a generous response to God's call to you to come up higher in your relationship with Him. After all, you will need tools to sharpen your spiritual life and keep it growing until you reach heaven, your ultimate destiny.

Worrying can sap your energy and weaken your relationship with, and trust in God. Are you the worrying type, or do you have burdens in your life right now that weigh you down and take most of the joy out of your life? Have you ever wondered if there is a solution or cure for worrying that always works? The good news is that there is a guaranteed way to get relief from your burdens and worries that works. Does this sound too good to be true? If I or someone else invented the method to help you stop worrying, then it might very well be too good to be true. But Jesus Christ, the Son of God, is the one offering us the solution to help us stop worrying and start making a lasting impact in our lives. Three Scripture passages provide the clue to Jesus' offer:

> "Come to Me all you who are weary and who are heavy laden, and I will give you rest. Take My yoke upon you and learn from Me, for I am gentle and humble of heart, and you will find rest for your souls. For My yoke is easy and My burden is light." (Mt 11:28-30)

"But seek first the kingdom of God and His righteousness, and all these things will be added to you." (Mt 6:33)

"Humble yourselves, therefore, under the mighty hand of God so that at the proper time He may exalt you, casting all your anxieties on Him, because He cares for you." (1 Pet 5:6-7)

These three Scripture passages say essentially the same thing, that is, stop worrying and trust that God knows and cares about your needs and your burdens. However, do we believe Jesus and take Him at His word? If we did, we would all be living much happier and worry-free lives. We know too well that this is not the case for most people. But it is not too late for us to learn the simple but profound truth that Jesus is trying to teach us here.

Let us focus on the first Scripture passage above, namely, Matthew 11:28-30, and discuss its deeper meaning. You might be wondering already from reading it why Jesus asks you in this Scripture passage to take His yoke upon you when you have come to Him with all your worries and heavy burdens. This might not make sense to you since you want relief from your problems, and you certainly did not come to Him, asking for more burdens to carry! There is a deeper meaning here to this Scripture passage, namely, that Jesus is asking you to give Him all your burdens and, in exchange, to take His easy yoke upon you. He wants you to enter into a deeper and more personal relationship with Him, instead of being wrapped up in your problems and burdens, depriving you of spending quality time with Him and caring for His more significant burdens. His burdens have everlasting consequences, whereas our burdens typically only matter while we are on this earth. He wants us to make better use of our time in this life and thus to make a difference for all eternity instead of getting wrapped up in our temporal problems. Research has shown that only eight percent of our worries are worth our genuine concern. Here is an authoritative estimate of what most people worry about:

- Things that never happen: 40%. That is, 40% of the things we worry about will never occur anyway.
- Things in the past that cannot be changed by all the worry in the world: 30%.
- Needless worries about our health: 12%.
- Petty, miscellaneous worries: 10%.
- Real, legitimate worries: 8%. Only 8% of our worries are worth our genuine concern. Ninety-two percent are pure fog with no substance at all.[28]

To illustrate how I came to discover the deeper meaning of the Scripture passage, Matthew 11:28-30, here is a true story that happened to me in Toronto, Canada, around 2006. I was running my own technology company AMH Communications, in which we served several high-profile and demanding customers. My employees and I were going through the toughest period that our company had experienced in many years. Three customers were experiencing critical computer problems on their respective networks. Even though I had some of the best technology consultants working for my company, they could not solve these three customers' problems no matter what they tried. The customers were becoming very upset with us. This was unusual for me to experience because my company had the reputation of being one of the best technology consulting firms to the legal vertical in Toronto. One morning, I got up early and started

---

[28] Earl Nightingale, *The Essence of Success* (www.bnpublishing.com).

The Key, The Door, and The Garden

my day with prayer, as was my habit. I told the Lord that I was feeling very burdened lately, and especially that morning. I asked Him to give me a passage from Scripture to help me overcome my burdens. I then randomly opened the Bible, and the page that lay open before me was Matthew chapter 11. My eyes fell on Matthew 11:28-30: *"Come to Me all you who are weary and who are heavy laden, and I will give you rest. Take My yoke upon you and learn from Me, for I am gentle and humble of heart, and you will find rest for your souls. For My yoke is easy and My burden is light."* I had read this passage many times before and thought I knew the meaning of it. But then I suddenly became confused; why was the Lord asking me to take His yoke upon me when I was already overburdened with my own problems? I asked the Lord to tell me what He was trying to teach me. Then I heard this gentle voice in my heart say to me: "Give Me your burdens." I said: "Lord, you know my burdens already, and anyway, they consist of worldly computer issues, which I don't think You really care about." He said: "I care about all of your problems, no matter what they are. Give me your burdens by naming them one at a time."

Hesitatingly, I named the first customer Merit Travel, and what the problem was - a software program that one of my software developers had written, which would stop working every morning without fail for the past three weeks when the technology manager tried to use it. We had sent the customer many software fixes to try to resolve the problem, but none of them had worked. The customer was losing patience quickly, and we were out of solutions. The Lord then told me to give Him this problem completely, to picture myself taking it out of my mind and my heart like a plant with all of its roots and then placing it into His open, capable hands. He did not allow me to name the next problem until I had completely stopped worrying and thinking about this first customer problem. When I was ready a few minutes later, He asked me to name the next customer and its situation. I told Him that the customer was WeirFoulds LLP. The problem was that for over one month, all 200 computers on their network were experiencing intermittent slowdowns. By midday every day, at least ten users' computers were dropping off the network entirely. Those users had to log back into their computers, causing them frustration and wasted productivity. We had placed sophisticated network monitoring equipment on their network for a few weeks to pinpoint the problem but to no avail.

Again, the Lord said to me to give Him this problem completely, to picture myself taking it out of my mind and my heart, and then placing it into His open hands. I did this, and I was now starting to feel less burdened. Finally, after a few more minutes, I moved on to tell the Lord about the third customer Stikeman Elliott LLP, and their issue - a computer script that I had written, which was not doing what it was supposed to do. I had tried many fixes, but none of them had worked. Again, the Lord said to me to completely give Him this problem by placing it into His open hands. After a few more minutes, I did this and felt completely unburdened, and I experienced a lightness, almost like a child. What a feeling - all my worries were entirely gone after about 10 minutes of prayer!

Then the Lord said to me: "Now it's your turn to take My yoke upon you." I said: "Lord, what is your main burden?" He said: "My main burden is seeing so many of My children lose their souls for all eternity. The loss of even one soul to hell plunges Me into the deepest sorrow. I want you to pray for the conversion of sinners." Right then, with an *unburdened* heart and mind, I started praying fervently for the conversion of sinners, and especially those who were most in danger of losing their souls that day. My prayer came right from the heart, and I was even crying as I prayed for these souls. I continued praying for about ten more minutes. Even when my prayer time came to an end that morning, I continued to remember these souls throughout my workday when I had spare time, such as driving to visit these three customers.

As my workday started, I called the technology manager at Merit Travel. I asked him to provide me with a status update on the software program that kept locking up whenever he tried to use it. He said that strangely enough, he came into his office that morning and launched the program, and it started normally. Furthermore, it had not frozen at all that morning, which was the first time that had happened in three weeks. I asked him if he had rebooted the computer on which that software program was running, and he said no. I then asked him if our leading software developer had sent him a software fix that morning or the day before, and he said no. I asked him to confirm once more that nothing had changed from yesterday when he left work to this morning when he came in, and he said that was correct. I asked him in disbelief to confirm that the software program was now working correctly, and he said yes. I told him thanks for the update, and he sounded relieved and happy that the program was now mysteriously working, and then I hung up the phone in total shock. Then I heard a gentle voice inside of me say: "I told you that I would take care of your problems better and faster than you could."

Next, I arrived at WeirFoulds LLP and had a meeting with the technology manager to discuss the network slowdown problem. He said that strangely no such issues had been reported by any of the 200 users all morning, and it was already 2:00 PM in the afternoon. I asked if my senior technology consultant had done anything the day before or that morning to repair the problem, and he said no. I told him thanks for the update, and he was also relieved and happy that the network was now functioning correctly, and I left the meeting again in shock. Then I heard a little voice inside of me say: "Are you now starting to believe Me when I told you that I would take care of your problems?" I said: "Lord, You never cease to amaze me. You even know how to solve earthly computer problems. I thought You were more interested in our spiritual problems."

Finally, I arrived at Stikeman Elliott LLP and had a meeting with one of their application specialists to discuss the script I had written a month ago. He showed me the software code, and suddenly, an idea came to me as to how to fix it. Within minutes, I had the script working, and he thanked me for finally fixing this issue, which had been ongoing for a few weeks. By now, it was 3:00 PM, and my day was over early. It was an entirely successful day, with all three customers happy with all my problems solved! I also felt good that I had been praying during the day when I found time, for the conversion of sinners and that I was helping Jesus carry His burdens, as He had helped me carry mine that day. Then I heard the gentle voice inside of me say: "Do you now believe Me when I told you that I would take care of all your problems?" I said: "Lord, I believe You now! I now understand the true meaning of Matthew 11:28-30. It is about entering into a deeper and more trusting relationship with You, isn't it?" He said: "Yes, My child. I desire you to share your problems with Me no matter what they are and for you to take concern for My burdens with a free and loving heart. Do not consume all your energy worrying about earthly problems that are of little consequence in the life to come. Rather, concern yourself with spiritual problems, especially the ones that have everlasting consequences, like the difference between souls going to heaven instead of hell!"

Thus, the passage from Matthew 11:28-30 is all about deepening your relationship with Jesus. What the Lord wants you and I to do is to name our burdens for Him one by one and to give them to Him entirely without holding back any of these burdens. You will know whether you have given Him your burdens entirely if you have ceased to think and worry about them. I invite you to try this with Jesus: think of your first burden and then picture yourself taking it out of your mind and out of your heart and putting it into the open hands of Jesus. Spend a few minutes visualizing yourself giving Jesus this burden. When you have stopped thinking about this burden anymore, and when it no longer occupies any of your thoughts or your emotions, then you know that you have given this burden over to Jesus. Then choose your next issue, do the same thing, and do not move on to the other burdens until you have given this burden completely to Him. Then do this for the rest of your burdens until your heart and mind are completely free of all your worries.

Now that your heart and mind are entirely free and available to Jesus, ask Him what His burdens are. He may say to you: "My main burden is seeing so many of My children lose their souls for all eternity, and so I want you to pray for the conversion of sinners." Or "I want you to pray for families that are in crisis." Or "I want you to pray for young people who seem to have lost their way and have a sense of hopelessness as they look to the future." Whatever you feel Jesus is asking you to pray for in your heart, spend the next few minutes, and even throughout the day when you have time, praying *fervently* from your heart for that intention. Offer your sufferings in union with your prayer and Jesus' suffering on the cross for that intention, and especially for the salvation of souls. Now you have genuinely taken Jesus' yoke upon you, which, as He said, is easy and light. You would have given the Lord your burdens, and taken His yoke upon your shoulders. You will begin to realize what the meaning of the scripture passage Matthew 11:28-30 is; it is all about entering a deeper relationship with Jesus. Instead of you carrying your burdens and not having time to concern yourself with His burdens, Jesus is inviting you to enter into a holy exchange of your burdens with His.

Now watch and see what happens with your burdens throughout the day. Jesus can never be outdone in charity. Because you have willingly, and with a free heart and mind, taken Jesus' burdens upon you, and you are praying deeply and fervently for His intentions, He will, without a doubt, take care of your problems better than you can. After all, Jesus is the creator of the universe, and He can deal with your burdens no matter what they are, much better than you can. He dealt with my client issues on that fateful day back in 2006 with my three customers, Merit Travel, WeirFoulds LLP, and Stikeman Elliott LLP. Incidentally, in case you are wondering, those problems never reoccurred with these three customers again. I have used the same technique with many of my problems since 2006. When I find myself worrying needlessly about some temporal problem, I stop and remind myself about what Jesus taught me back in 2006, and I give Jesus my burdens and carry His instead. My worries go away, and Jesus solves my problems better than I ever could myself. At the same time, I make a lasting difference with my life by praying for the salvation of souls who might otherwise have been lost that day if no one stood in the gap and prayed for them.

Now that is what I call a real solution to the problem of worrying, a complete "win-win-win" solution - Jesus' answer to worrying. It is a win for Jesus because He is happier that more souls have made it to heaven that day; it is a win for you because your problems have been solved by Jesus better than you could have solved them yourself, and you have helped Jesus to save souls, thus making a more lasting impact with your life. Finally, it is a win for those souls who are now in heaven instead of in hell!

What if my Problems Remain?

Will Jesus take away your problems every time you use the solution provided in the chapter? The answer is: not always, but there is still good news here. He will still take away your worries about your burdens, even if they remain as they are for the moment. He will assure you that He has done that for a reason; after all, He knows best and may be keeping these situations as they are to purify you and make you more dependent on His grace. He may be calling you to participate with Him in helping to save souls. However, I assure you that if you have faithfully exchanged burdens with Jesus, your worries will be gone, and you will even joyfully carry the burdens that remain in your life.

When Jesus is ready, He will remove these burdens, and you will understand His plan in all of this for your spiritual growth. Many Saints were joyful when the time for their martyrdom came. St. Lawrence joked with his executioners when he was being roasted alive over a fire. He said that they needed to turn him over because one side of him was already cooked! St. Ignatius of Antioch was destined to be thrown to the lions in a Roman colosseum, and he begged his followers not to intervene to stop his martyrdom. He wanted to be thoroughly chewed and ground up by the lions until nothing was left of him! Jesus did not remove the pending execution of these two Saints, but He substituted their worries with the joy of following in His footsteps and offering their lives for the salvation of souls.

Summary

The way you stop worrying is to completely give your problems to Jesus daily and then take His burdens in return. The passage from Matthew 11:28-30 is all about deepening your relationship with Jesus. What the Lord wants us to do is to name our burdens for Him one by one and to give them to Him entirely without holding back any of these burdens. You will know whether you have given Him your burdens entirely if you have ceased to think and worry about them. You will start making a real and lasting difference in other people's spiritual well-being by praying fervently for them. When these souls see you in heaven one day, they will thank you for all eternity for helping to save them from going to hell. Your life would then have been well spent and God-centered, and Jesus will then say to you: "Well done, good and faithful servant. Enter into the joy of your master's kingdom."

14 Let God Change Your Water into His Sweet Wine

Following the theme of the last chapter, I want to explore other ways to make offerings to God to help with the eternal well-being of other souls.

The Wedding at Cana

Let us recall the Scripture passage that details what happened at the wedding in Cana of Galilee. There is something profound about its spirituality and message for each one of us, especially those who do not hold significant positions of power and authority in society or in the Church, which represents the majority of the world's population:

> "On the third day there was a wedding at Cana in Galilee, and the Mother of Jesus was there. Jesus also was invited to the wedding with His disciples. When the wine ran out, the Mother of Jesus said to Him, "They have no wine." And Jesus said to Her, "Woman, what does this have to do with Me? My hour has not yet come." His mother said to the servants, "Do whatever He tells you." Now there were six stone water jars there for the Jewish rites of purification, each holding twenty or thirty gallons. Jesus said to the servants, "Fill the jars with water." And they filled them up to the brim. And He said to them, "Now draw some out and take it to the master of the feast." So they took it. When the master of the feast tasted the water now become wine, and did not know where it came from (though the servants who had drawn the water knew), the master of the feast called the bridegroom and said to him, "Everyone serves the good wine first, and when people have

drunk freely, then the poor wine. But you have kept the good wine until now." This, the first of His signs, Jesus did at Cana in Galilee, and manifested His glory. And His disciples believed in Him." (Jn 2:1-11)

There is the stunning miracle of Jesus changing ordinary water into the best-tasting wine that pleased everyone present and saved the bride and bridegroom from the embarrassment of running out of wine at their wedding. There is, however, a powerful underlying meaning for each one of us. This came to me one day in Toronto while I was praying the Luminous mysteries of the Rosary. The stone jars represent you and me, as we can often be heavy for God to lift up to Himself, and we are prone to getting chips (venial sins) and even holes (mortal sins) in our stone jars. These need to be repaired by repentance in the case of venial sins and by Sacramental Confession in the case of mortal sins for full reintegration into the sacramental life of the Church. Otherwise, our jars cannot hold water effectively and reliably.

The analogy of filing our stone jars with the "water" is akin to filling our lives with:

- Prayer with the heart
- Work done out of love for Jesus
- Suffering offered up in union with Jesus' sufferings
- Silence
- Sacraments

We then ask Jesus to bless that "water" and change it into the sweet tasting "wine" of His supernatural graces and blessings for others. His angels (like the servants in the wedding at Cana) will then draw some graces (wine) out of our stone jars and give those graces to whoever needs them most, people unknown to us until we reach heaven.

The "Little Way"

The above analogy is similar to the "Little Way"[29] espoused by St. Thérèse of Lisieux, also known affectionately as "the Little Flower." All she did in her life was to scrub the convent floors and take care of the older nuns in the convent, all while suffering hiddenly from tuberculosis. Her mantra was: "I may not be able to do great things, but I can do small things out of great love for Jesus."

Preaching brilliant sermons, writing best-selling books, and performing miracles in Jesus' name are admirable actions. However, our desire and commitment to stand with Mary and John at the foot of the cross daily, offering up our sufferings to God the Father in union with Jesus' sufferings on the cross for the salvation of the world might be even more admirable. When others make us suffer and put us on grievous crosses, we should try to rectify the grievances, but f all our efforts fail, then we must accept these crosses, and forgive those who have placed us there. This action of a Christian that he or she can practice daily is most valuable in God's eyes. It produces invisible but powerful graces that God can give to the souls of people unknown to us. These graces can bring about their permanent and life-altering conversion, often more so than sermons, books, and miracles performed. The Apostle St. Paul taught us this when he said: "Now I rejoice in my sufferings for your sake, and in my flesh, I am

---

[29] Thérèse of Lisieux Staff, *The Little Way of St. Thérèse of Lisieux: In Her Own Words* (Catholic Truth Society, 2009).

filling up what is lacking in Christ's afflictions for the sake of his body, that is, the church" (Col 1:24).

If you sincerely believe that this "Little Way" to achieve holiness is available to everyone without exception, then you will be on your way to becoming a saint yourself! When St. John Paul II declared St. Thérèse of Lisieux a Doctor of the Church in 1997, I was most surprised. She had not written any volumes of theology like many of the previously declared Doctors of the Church. These include St. Thomas Aquinas, St. Ambrose, St. Augustine, St. Gregory the Great, St. Athanasius, and the list goes on (there are a total of 37 Doctors of the Church). I could not figure out why such a learned and saintly pope like John Paull II would think that St. Thérèse had something so profound to offer the Church as to make her a Doctor. Then one day, it dawned on me why this wise pope did what he did. Most people in the world will never become priests, bishops, cardinals, popes, prime ministers, presidents, or CEOs of companies. Most of us are considered "little" in the eyes of society. Does that mean that we cannot achieve holiness and become Saints one day, even great Saints at that? St. Thérèse emphatically answered that question for us by showing us her "Little Way" to holiness. Ironically, she always wanted to be a missionary and to be considered someone important in the Church. When she entered the Carmelite convent in France at the tender age of 15, she wrestled with finding her unique place in the Church. She had an ardent desire to give the Church something substantial as a gift. She lamented that she could not be like the Church's great Saints, such as the great missionary Apostle St. Paul and others. One day while praying about this, she was led to this Scripture passage:

Let God Change Your Water into His Sweet Wine

"If I speak in the tongues of men and of angels, but have not love, I am a noisy gong or a clanging cymbal. And if I have prophetic powers, and understand all mysteries and all knowledge, and if I have all faith, so as to remove mountains, but have not love, I am nothing. If I give away all I have, and if I deliver up my body to be burned, but have not love, I gain nothing. Love is patient and kind; love does not envy or boast; it is not arrogant or rude. It does not insist on its own way; it is not irritable or resentful; it does not rejoice at wrongdoing but rejoices with the truth. Love bears all things, believes all things, hopes all things, endures all things. Love never ends. As for prophecies, they will pass away; as for tongues, they will cease; as for knowledge, it will pass away. For we know in part and we prophesy in part, but when the perfect comes, the partial will pass away. When I was a child, I spoke like a child, I thought like a child, I reasoned like a child. When I became a man, I gave up childish ways. For now we see in a mirror dimly, but then face to face. Now I know in part; then I shall know fully, even as I have been fully known. So now faith, hope, and love abide, these three; but the greatest of these is love" (1 Cor 13).

Then it dawned on her that she had found her place in the Church. She was called to do small things out of great love! What a simple but profound theology that can be lived by anyone. She dared to say that it was the shortest and easiest way to holiness – the way of love. That is why St. John Paul II realized that, while her theology of the "Little Way" was simple, it applied to 99.9% of the world. Now, it is up to you and me to take up the challenge of living the "Little Way" and doing everything out of great love for Jesus. St. Thérèse once said that if you pick up a pin from the floor out of love for Jesus, you can help to save one soul. How about taking out the garbage every day out of love for Jesus? How about offering up the inconvenience of being stuck in traffic for love of Jesus, or living with a difficult spouse, raising a challenging child, or dealing with an unpleasant work environment? The list is endless, but you get the point. All these situations are ways to fill your stone jar with water and ask Jesus to change it into His wine for your fellowman.

I have realized something amazing that happens every time I practice the "Little Way" in my daily life. I gain great joy and purpose when I offer up out of love for Jesus, everything I do, or anything unpleasant that happens to me. Many times, the suffering of the situation that I offer up to Jesus seems to be lessened. There is a saying: "God cannot be outdone in charity." If you have just offered up some suffering or inconvenience out of love for Jesus, which will help save a soul or two (or even more), then Jesus will surely reward you in the next life, and very often He rewards you in this life. Now, you must be careful that you are not just offering up your suffering or daily tasks to get an immediate reward from Jesus. You must do it out of pure and disinterested love and then leave any consolations up to Jesus. But trust me, He cannot be outdone in charity.

The Parable of the Ten Virgins

Let us examine the parable of the ten virgins, the five wise ones, and the five foolish ones.

> Then the kingdom of heaven will be like ten virgins who took their lamps and went to meet the bridegroom. Five of them were foolish, and five were wise. For when the foolish took their lamps, they took no oil with them, but the wise took flasks of oil with

their lamps. As the bridegroom was delayed, they all became drowsy and slept. But at midnight there was a cry, 'Here is the bridegroom! Come out to meet him.' Then all those virgins rose and trimmed their lamps. And the foolish said to the wise, 'Give us some of your oil, for our lamps are going out.' But the wise answered, saying, 'Since there will not be enough for us and for you, go rather to the dealers and buy for yourselves.' And while they were going to buy, the bridegroom came, and those who were ready went in with him to the marriage feast, and the door was shut. Afterward the other virgins came also, saying, 'Lord, lord, open to us.' But he answered, 'Truly, I say to you, I do not know you.' Watch therefore, for you know neither the day nor the hour. (Mt 25:1-13)

The oil in the lamps of the virgins represents the effect of prayer on our souls. As oil, when lit in a lamp, causes it to radiate light for the one with the lamp as well as for those around him or her, so prayer in our souls radiates a spiritual light to guide us and those in our lives.

You cannot easily give your deep prayer life and spirituality to someone else instantly when they ask you for it. This primarily occurs in times of crisis when people who have not built up their prayer life over the years suddenly experience a problem that takes them by surprise. They come to others who have a deep prayer life and hence lots of spare "oil" in their lamps, and they want to get some of their peace and calm immediately. Unfortunately, it does not work that way. That is what happened to the five foolish virgins in the parable of the ten virgins. The wise virgins told them to go to the dealers and buy oil for themselves, and by the time they came back from the dealers, the marriage feast was closed to them.

The Key, The Door, and The Garden

There are so many forms of dissipative activities in our world today that people engage in, with the technology revolution driving many of them. Others include an excessive attachment to sports, entertainment, games of chance, and the list goes on. We must have the discipline to put these things in their respective places in our lives and not be like the five foolish virgins. We will reap what we sow. A deep prayer life will give us inner joy, peace, and strength, especially in times of trials. Likewise, a lack of prayer will lead to a life that lacks balance and grace. This was obvious to see in late 2019 and onward when the Coronavirus pandemic struck the world by surprise. The "wise virgins" remained calm and without fear, while the "foolish virgins" panicked and will probably stay in a state of anxiety until the pandemic completely disappears. But then another crisis is always lurking around the corner.

Summary

The moral of this chapter is: fill your stone jar with water and, with the eyes of faith, see God's wine being given to others in need of God's graces. You will then be filled with supernatural peace and joy daily, and you will be giving your life such meaning and purpose that when you get to heaven one day (God willing), you will look back and say: why did I not fill my stone jar with even more "water"? Remember, the "water" represents prayer, work, silence, suffering, and the Sacraments, which I like to abbreviate PWSSS because it makes it easy to remember.

Try to also live the "Little Way" espoused by St. Thérèse of Lisieux. Her mantra was: "I may not be able to do great things, but I can do small things out of great love for Jesus."

15 The Holy Mass and the Eucharist – The Summit

Following the analogy from the last chapter of oil for our lamps, there is a very high-quality "oil" that we can use as Christians. The title of this chapter should have caught your attention because summit means the top of a mountain. To understand what the Eucharist is, you must believe with all your heart that it is a Person, you must receive the Eucharist regularly, and then you will find yourself becoming over time like that Person who you are receiving. That Person is the God-man, Jesus Christ, who gave us the great gift of the Eucharist at the Last Supper, the day before He died on the cross at Calvary. Simply put, the Eucharist is the Body, Blood, Soul, and Divinity of Jesus Christ. He gave us this great gift of Himself to strengthen us on our Christian journey through this life because He knew it would be difficult for us to live all of the teachings He left us to follow.

Let us face facts: who finds it easy to forgive one's enemies? Who finds it easy to turn the other cheek? Who finds it easy to love all men and women as Jesus loves us? Who finds it easy to suffer, not to complain, and to offer up their suffering in union with Jesus' suffering for the salvation of souls? Who finds it easy to persevere until the end while trying to live all of Jesus' difficult teachings? If you think you can, then you are either superhuman, or you are deceiving yourself! I would instead think it is the latter.

The Holy Mass (more fully known as the Holy Sacrifice of the Mass) is the re-creation of Jesus' sacrifice on Calvary made present to us in our time. Here is another way of saying this: the veil of time is torn in two, and you and I are transported back in time to be present at Jesus' crucifixion. Does this sound too good to be true or too strange to believe? Remember that with God, all things are possible.

The Key, The Door, and The Garden

A person living in our time could argue that he or she was not present at Jesus' sacrifice on Calvary and does not have the full or direct benefits it brought to the world. This includes payment owed to the Father for all the sins ever committed in the past and will ever be committed in the future. Jesus anticipated your complaint, and that is why He instituted the Eucharist at the first Mass on Holy Thursday. Remember this: whenever the Holy Sacrifice of the Mass is being celebrated in any given town or city, that is the most incredible event happening in the world at that time. It is more significant than any other show or concert on earth. If only we could see with the eyes of heaven what occurs at Holy Mass, we would fall prostrate in worship and amazement. We would see Our Lady and the angels present on the altar, worshipping Jesus as He offers Himself for the salvation of the world!

The most definitive proof that Jesus wanted to give us His flesh to eat and His blood to drink comes from St. John's Gospel, chapter 6. Jesus stated seven times that we must eat His flesh and drink His blood if we want to have His life in us. Incidentally, in Scripture, seven often symbolizes completion or perfection. Genesis tells us that God created the heavens and the Earth in six days, and, upon completion, God rested on the seventh day. This stresses how much Jesus wanted us to believe this teaching on the Eucharist. Here is a fraction of chapter 6 of St. John's Gospel, but I strongly encourage you to read all of chapter 6:

> The Jews then disputed among themselves, saying, "How can this man give us His flesh to eat?" So Jesus said to them, "Truly, truly, I say to you, unless you eat the flesh of the Son of Man and drink His blood, you have no life in you. Whoever feeds on My flesh and drinks My blood has eternal life, and I will raise him up on

the last day. For My flesh is true food, and My blood is true drink. Whoever feeds on My flesh and drinks My blood abides in Me, and I in him. As the living Father sent Me, and I live because of the Father, so whoever feeds on Me, he also will live because of Me. This is the bread that came down from heaven, not like the bread the fathers ate, and died. Whoever feeds on this bread will live forever." Jesus said these things in the synagogue, as he taught at Capernaum. (Jn 6:52-59).

After this many of his disciples turned back and no longer walked with him. So Jesus said to the twelve, "Do you want to go away as well?" Simon Peter answered him, "Lord, to whom shall we go? You have the words of eternal life, and we have believed, and have come to know, that You are the Holy One of God." (Jn 6:66-69)

A line in the above Scripture passage is worth exploring because it is somewhat shocking: "Truly, truly, I say to you, unless you eat the flesh of the Son of Man and drink his blood, you have no life in you." You might argue that you have either never received the Eucharist in your life, or you no longer receive it, or you receive it but do not believe that Jesus is truly present in the Eucharist. Yet, you have life because you are breathing, eating, sleeping, going to work, and even having "fun" in your life. What Jesus was referring to was divine life in your soul. You still have your human life, but you do not have God's life infused into your soul. If you continue along that path, you may very well get to the end of your life and find yourself excluded from the kingdom of God. That is why the Eucharist is described as a foretaste of heaven.

Some people have argued that Jesus was only using symbolic language in John, chapter 6 and that He did not mean for us literally

The Key, The Door, and The Garden

to eat His body and drink His blood. If that was the case, then why did Jesus not stop those "many disciples" from turning away from Him when He gave this teaching? Jesus could easily have said to them not to go away because He was only using symbolic language. However, He did not back down from His teaching and was even willing to lose His twelve chosen Apostles! The Apostles did not understand why Jesus needed to give them His body and blood as food and drink. However, they stayed with Him, accepted His teaching, partook of the Eucharist at the Last Supper, and then saw Jesus consummate His gift by dying on the cross the next day.

I would also like to give a gory example to illustrate why Jesus left us the Eucharist. I quote David Scheimann here as he describes one of the practices of some of the early First Nations peoples ("Indians" in his text):

> All of the Indian tribes believe that every object, animate or inanimate, has a spirit. The Iroquois held the belief that to eat a thing is to gain its power. This follows naturally from the previous view, because even in death the body's remains keep at least part of its soul.
>
> They believed that devouring the flesh of a great warrior would transfer his prowess into the one doing the eating. There is no mention that the Iroquois ate the flesh of those captives who did not die ceremoniously; perhaps these "weak" prisoners were considered unworthy to be eaten. There is also no mention that the Iroquois ate the flesh of anyone who was not tortured to death - those people who did not have a chance to prove themselves. Yet like the previous spiritual explanation, only one account exists that establishes a link between great warriors and the humans they eat. A Huron Indian who escaped Iroquois captivity described how a

Jesuit was killed and eaten. The priest had endured great pain before his death, and the Iroquois told the Huron that they drank his blood and ate his flesh so that they could be as strong as the priest had been.[30]

Similarly, if you eat Jesus' flesh and drink His blood regularly, over time, you will become as strong a warrior as He was.

The Catechism of the Catholic Church teaches the following on the Eucharist:

The holy Eucharist completes Christian initiation. Those who have been raised to the dignity of the royal priesthood by Baptism and configured more deeply to Christ by Confirmation participate with the whole community in the Lord's own sacrifice by means of the Eucharist.

At the Last Supper, on the night he was betrayed, our Saviour instituted the Eucharistic sacrifice of his Body and Blood. This he did in order to perpetuate the sacrifice of the cross throughout the ages until he should come again, and so to entrust to his beloved Spouse, the Church, a memorial of his death and resurrection: a sacrament of love, a sign of unity, a bond of charity, a Paschal banquet in which Christ is consumed, the mind is filled with grace, and a pledge of future glory is given to us.

The Eucharist is the source and summit of the Christian life. The other sacraments, and indeed all ecclesiastical ministries and works of the apostolate, are bound up with the Eucharist and are oriented toward it. For in the blessed Eucharist is contained the

---

[30] David Scheimann, *Adoption or Entrée* (Ohio University: https://www.ohio.edu/orgs/glass/vol/1/14.htm).

whole spiritual good of the Church, namely Christ himself, our Pasch.

The Eucharist is the efficacious sign and sublime cause of that communion in the divine life and that unity of the People of God by which the Church is kept in being. It is the culmination both of God's action sanctifying the world in Christ and of the worship men offer to Christ and through him to the Father in the Holy Spirit.

Finally, by the Eucharistic celebration we already unite ourselves with the heavenly liturgy and anticipate eternal life, when God will be all in all.[31]

A Pew Research Center survey conducted in 2019 in the United States found that "most self-described Catholics do not believe in this core teaching. Nearly seven-in-ten Catholics (69%) say they personally believe that during Catholic Mass, the bread and wine used in Communion are symbols of the body and blood of Jesus Christ. Just one-third of U.S. Catholics (31%) say they believe that during Catholic Mass, the bread and wine actually become the body and blood of Jesus."[32]

Sadly, even though the above survey was conducted in the US, the same rough statistics apply to Catholics in most countries. Add to that fact that most Protestants do not believe that the Eucharist is truly the Body, Blood, Soul, and Divinity of Jesus Christ. Finally, add to the above two groups, people of all other non-Christian religions and, of course, atheists who do not believe in Jesus at all. This equates

---

[31] *Catechism of the Catholic Church, Second Edition* (Libreria Editrice Vaticana, 1994, 1997), no. 1322-1326.

[32] *Pew Study* (5 August 2019).

to only five percent of the entire world's population who believe in one of the most incredible gift ever left on earth by God's Son, Jesus Christ. The other 95% of the world's population are missing out on spiritual nourishment par excellence.

Here is another great passage from Scripture that demonstrates how powerfully Jesus is present in the Eucharist. It is the story of the two disciples leaving Jerusalem after Jesus' crucifixion and traveling along the road to Emmaus. They were despondent because they did not understand why Jesus did not use His divine power to stop Himself from being captured and put to death by the Romans. They were so despondent that they left the group of Apostles and other disciples and were wandering away in the night. "So they drew near to the village to which they were going. He acted as if He were going farther, but they urged Him strongly, saying, "Stay with us, for it is toward evening and the day is now far spent." So He went in to stay with them. When He was at table with them, He took the bread and blessed and broke it and gave it to them. And their eyes were opened, and they recognized Him. And He vanished from their sight" (Lk 24:28-31).

You should believe in the real presence of Jesus in the Eucharist because all the canonized Saints of the Catholic Church over the past 2,000 years fully believed in the real presence of Jesus in the Eucharist. Remember, these Saints lived heroically holy lives, and each of them performed or continues to perform miracles from heaven for those who pray and ask for their intercession before the throne of God. If you do not believe in the real presence of Jesus in the Eucharist, then you either consider these Saints to be wrong in their belief and that you are right in yours, or you do not care one way or the other to debate the subject. Both of these approaches do not bode well for the eternal destiny of your soul.

The Key, The Door, and The Garden

Eucharistic Miracles

I would like to share with you a Eucharistic miracle that happened to me personally in Canada around 2005. I had suffered from stomach problems since I was a child after having contracted severe gastroenteritis. I frequently experienced stomach pains throughout my childhood, teenage years, and young adult life. If I did not eat my meals on time, I would pay dearly for not doing so, and I would suffer stomach pains, which would only gradually subside by the end of that day. Things took a turn for the worse in my early forties when I missed eating lunch one day, followed by drinking a carbonated beverage at dinner. The ensuing battle with severe stomach acid and pains lasted over a year and even led to atrial fibrillation while trying to sleep at night. I had tried the most potent stomach medications available, and all known natural remedies, but the pain was only slightly reduced.

Around the same period in my life, I was an extraordinary minister of Holy Communion to the sick and elderly in Toronto, Canada. I had been taking Holy Communion to patients in hospitals and at a residence for the elderly for over 15 years. One particular Sunday was memorable for what happened. When I went to Mass at St. Justin Martyr Parish, it was my turn to take Holy Communion to the home for the elderly. I went up to the altar at Communion time, received the Eucharist, and was given approximately ten Hosts in a golden pyx to give to the elderly residents at that home. I placed the pyx in the carrying case and then put the carrying case with its string around my neck, as was customary. I then got into my car and started driving to the home for the elderly. It was a short drive, no more than five minutes away. The pyx in its carrying case was resting directly on my stomach. Then I heard a gentle voice within me say: "Claim the healing." I replied: "What healing?" The voice replied: "The healing of your stomach because I am resting on your stomach in the Eucharist." I then replied: "Lord, I claim the healing of my stomach." That very same day, my stomach was completely and miraculously healed of all pain and discomfort, and I have never had to take any stomach medications since. That was in 2005, and I am happy to say that I can eat anything I want to, no matter how spicy or hot. I no longer have to eat my meals on time, and I can even skip meals. The healing was so thorough and miraculous that I once fasted for three days only on the Eucharist and water. That would have been unheard of before my healing.

There have been many documented Eucharistic miracles down through the centuries, with the most famous one being the Miracle of Lanciano. The Miracle of Lanciano is a Eucharistic miracle alleged to have occurred in the eighth century in Lanciano, Italy. According to tradition, a monk who had doubts about the real presence of Christ in the Eucharist found, when he said the words of consecration at Mass, that the bread and wine changed into flesh and blood. The Catholic Church officially claims the miracle as authentic. Today, you can visit the city of Lanciano and observe the piece of flesh enclosed in a monstrance.

Proper Preparation for Receiving the Eucharist

We need to be in a state of grace for the Eucharist to have a positive effect on our souls. Chapter 5 of this book deals with how we can determine to a relatively strong degree of certainty if we are currently in a state of grace or not. The Church teaches that any Catholic Christian with mortal sin on their soul cannot and should not receive

The Key, The Door, and The Garden

Holy Communion. The Church also teaches that non-Catholics cannot receive Holy Communion until they are officially catechized and join the Catholic Church. Otherwise, you run the risk of the Eucharist having a negative effect on your soul and not the positive impact you are expecting. St. Paul warns us: "For as often as you eat this bread and drink the cup, you proclaim the Lord's death until he comes. Whoever, therefore, eats the bread or drinks the cup of the Lord in an unworthy manner will be guilty concerning the body and blood of the Lord. Let a person examine himself, then, and so eat of the bread and drink of the cup. For anyone who eats and drinks without discerning the body eats and drinks judgment on himself. That is why many of you are weak and ill, and some have died" (1 Cor 11:26-30).

It is sad to see how many Catholics miss Mass for many Sundays in a row for no good reason (health problems or family emergencies), and yet when they go to Mass next, they casually walk up the aisle and receive the Eucharist. This is quite common with non-practicing Catholics who attend weddings or funerals and have nevertheless not been to Mass in months or even years. They simply believe that it is their right to receive the Eucharist without first going to Confession. We should all make an adequate examination of conscience before Mass and determine with a fair degree of accuracy if our souls might be in a state of mortal sin. Have we willingly and with full knowledge broken one or more of the Ten Commandments since we last went to Confession? If so, we are probably in a state of mortal sin and should not receive the Eucharist until we first go to Confession.

Eucharistic Adoration

A small percentage of Catholic Churches around the world offer what is known as Perpetual Eucharistic Adoration. Essentially, Jesus in the Blessed Sacrament is placed in a monstrance inside a chapel 24 hours a day, seven days a week, and worshipers can visit and pray to Him there. The parish has to commit to having at least one person, preferably two, on duty for every hour of the day. This takes a serious commitment from the parishioners, but the blessings that God gives that parish are incredible. Suppose the Catholic Church nearest you does not have Perpetual Eucharistic Adoration. In that case, you can always enter the Church and pray to Jesus, who is always reposed in the tabernacle of every Catholic Church. He will reward you now, especially in eternity, for every visit you have ever made to Him in front of the Blessed Sacrament.

Profound Insights from St. Peter Julian Eymard

Finally, I would like to leave you with some profound insights from one of the greatest writers on the Eucharist, St. Peter Julian Eymard (1811 – 1868). He was a French Catholic priest and founder of two religious institutes: the Congregation of the Blessed Sacrament for men and the Servants of the Blessed Sacrament for women.

Many people (and even Catholics) find it hard to believe that Jesus Christ is fully and truly present in the small white host: Body, Blood, Soul, and Divinity. St. Peter Julian Eymard gives us some profound reasons why Jesus chose to disguise Himself in this way to be our Emmanuel, "God with us." After you read these reasons, you will find yourself feeling ashamed that you misjudged Jesus and why He chose to stay with us in this simple and humble way until the end of time:

The Key, The Door, and The Garden

Express your wonder at the sacrifices He imposes on Himself in His sacramental state. He conceals the glory of His Divinity and humanity so as not to blind you. He veils His majesty that you may dare come to Him and speak to Him as friend to friend. He binds His power so as not to frighten or punish you. He does not manifest the perfection of His virtues so as not to discourage your weakness. He even checks the ardour of His Heart and of His love for you because you could not stand the strength and tenderness of it. He lets you see only His goodness, which filters through, as it were, and escapes from the Sacred Species like a ray of sunshine through a thin cloud.

How kind indeed is our sacramental Jesus. He welcomes you at any hour of the day or night. His love never knows rest. He is always most gentle toward you. When you visit Him, He forgets your sins and imperfections, and speaks only of His joy, His tenderness, and His love. By the reception He gives you, one would think that He has need of you to make Him happy.[33]

On the Eucharist meeting our every need, he brings home the point by vivid imagery:

O happy moment of Communion which makes us forget our exile and its miseries! O sweet repose of the soul on the very Heart of Jesus!

This good Master knows very well that we need to taste the sweetness of love now and then! One cannot always be on the

---

[33] St. Peter Julian Eymard, *The Real Presence* (Veritatis Splendor Publications, 2013), 28.

Calvary of suffering, nor in the thick of battle. The child needs the mother's bosom; the Christian, the Heart of Jesus.

Yes, virtue without Communion is like the strength of the lion; it is the result of combat, of violence; it is hard. If it is to have the gentleness of the Lamb, we must drink the Blood of the spotless Lamb; we must eat this honey of the desert.[34]

St. Peter also comments that our spirit will find joy in Communion:

In Communion, we enjoy our Lord in our Lord Himself. It is then that we have our most intimate communion with Him – a communion from which we gain a true and profound knowledge of what He is. It is then that Jesus manifests Himself to us most clearly. Faith is a light; Communion is at once light and feeling.

This manifestation of Jesus through Communion enlightens the mind and gives it a special aptitude for discerning more and more clearly the things of God.

It is the mystery of Emmaus re-enacted. When Jesus taught the two disciples along the way, explaining the Scriptures to them, their faith still wavered, although they felt inwardly some mysterious emotion. But by their participating in the breaking of the bread, immediately their eyes were opened, and their hearts were ready to burst with joy. The voice of Jesus had not sufficed to reveal His presence to them. They had to feel His Heart; they had to be fed with the Bread of understanding![35]

---

[34] St. Peter Julian Eymard, *How to Get More out of Holy Communion* (Sophia Institute Press, 2000), 14.

[35] Ibid, 28.

St. Peter shows us how Communion reveals God's love for us:

> The more you receive Communion, the more will your love be kindled, your heart enlarged; your affections will become more and more ardent and tender as the intensity of this divine fire increases. Jesus bestows upon us the grace of His love. He comes Himself to kindle this flame of love in our hearts. He feeds us by His frequent visits until it becomes a consuming fire.[36]

Summary

The Eucharist is the Body, Blood, Soul, and Divinity of Jesus Christ. He gave us this great gift of Himself to strengthen us on our Christian journey through this life because He knew it would be difficult for us to live all of the teachings that He left us to follow. The Holy Sacrifice of the Mass is the re-creation of the sacrifice Calvary made present in our time. Whenever the Holy Sacrifice of the Mass is being celebrated in any given town or city, that is the most incredible event happening in the world at that time. It is greater than any other show or concert on earth. If only we could see with the eyes of heaven what was occurring at Holy Mass, we would fall prostrate in worship and amazement.

---

[36] Ibid, 38.

16 Prayer with the Heart, Especially the Holy Rosary

Do you know what the definition of prayer is? Most people today would not be able to give an accurate answer. Here it is: "Prayer is the raising of one's heart and mind to God or the requesting of good things from God." Sounds so simple, right? I would guess that most people when they finish "praying," have not accomplished both the raising of their hearts *and* their minds to God. They probably have not done so for a sufficiently long period to walk away being filled with God's grace, joy, and peace and with the strength to face whatever their day is about to bring. You will recall from chapter 1 (God Exists, Guaranteed - From Atheist to Believer) that the author's survey in May 2020 revealed that 90% of respondents spend less than half an hour in prayer before starting their day, and approximately 65% spend less than ten minutes.

In the chapter entitled "The Key," I mentioned that if you do not meet God every morning before beginning your day, you will spend the rest of your day looking for Him in those you meet and in those with whom you interact. You will be left disappointed and empty because no one can take the place of God. This is one of the most significant causes of broken relationships, idolatry, addictions, and sin in the world.

The Catechism of the Catholic Church states clearly what prayer is, and the right disposition needed for prayer:

"Prayer is the raising of one's mind and heart to God or the requesting of good things from God." But when we pray, do we speak from the height of our pride and will, or "out of the depths" of a humble and contrite heart? He who humbles himself will be exalted; humility is the foundation of prayer. Only when we humbly acknowledge that "we do not know how to pray as we ought," are we ready to receive freely the gift of prayer. "Man is a beggar before God."[37]

In Jesus' dialog with the Samaritan woman at the well, He told her: "But the hour is coming, and is now here, when the true worshipers will worship the Father in spirit and truth, for the Father is seeking such people to worship Him. God is spirit, and those who worship Him must worship in spirit and truth" (Jn 4:23-24). You and I have often heard the phrase: "I am spiritual but not religious." Unfortunately, that contradicts what Jesus told the Samaritan woman about how to pray and worship God. You cannot merely worship God with whatever information and notions you have about God in your head. You might very well be fervent and be engaging your heart during your prayer time, but if it is not based on the truth about who God is, then your prayer falls short of the mark. We often then wonder why our prayers go unanswered. If that is the case with you, ask yourself if you are worshipping God in spirit *and* truth. We must make sure that we are praying to and following Jesus of Nazareth and not our invention of who we think Jesus is or should be.

There is also the opposite type of person who is religious but not very spiritual. This type of person knows the truth about God and His Son Jesus and knows all of the Church's teachings. However, they do not display the fruits of the Holy Spirit in their daily lives (charity, generosity, joy, gentleness, peace, faithfulness, patience, modesty, kindness, self-control, goodness, and chastity).

---

[37] *Catechism of the Catholic Church, Second Edition* (Libreria Editrice Vaticana, 1994, 1997), no. 2559.

Prayer with the Heart, Especially the Holy Rosary

When we finish our time of prayer, we should be able to say like the aged Simeon: "Lord, now you are letting your servant depart in peace, according to your word; for my eyes have seen your salvation that you have prepared in the presence of all peoples, a light for revelation to the Gentiles, and for glory to your people Israel" (Lk 2:29-32).

Regarding the need to pray always, Jesus advised us: "Therefore, stay awake, for you do not know on what day your Lord is coming" (Mt 24:42). St. Paul also advises us: "Rejoice always, pray without ceasing, give thanks in all circumstances; for this is the will of God in Christ Jesus for you" (1 Thess 5:16-18).

Our Lady of Medjugorje has been tireless in asking us to not just pray with our lips and our minds, but most importantly, to pray with our hearts. In two separate messages to the visionaries of Medjugorje, Our Lady first said: "Pray until prayer becomes a joy." More recently, She said: "Pray until prayer becomes your life." If I had to summarize Our Lady's call to us from Medjugorje, I would use the above two messages because She is essentially trying to teach us to become more like Her in our spiritual lives and in our relationship with God. After all, She was and is the Woman of prayer. Can you imagine a moment during Her earthly life when She was not praying? I sincerely believe that even while She was performing Her daily chores around Her home in Nazareth, She would have been praying and offering up Her work to God as a sacrifice. Can you imagine the kind of person you or I would become if we prayed until prayer became our lives? Then imagine the kind of world we would have if everyone prayed until prayer became their lives. Nothing short of a paradise!

The Key, The Door, and The Garden

The Lord's Prayer

The greatest and most sublime prayer ever taught to the human race was the Lord's prayer. Jesus said:

Pray then like this:

"Our Father in heaven,
hallowed be Your name.
Your kingdom come,
Your will be done,
on earth as it is in heaven.
Give us this day our daily bread,
and forgive us our debts,
as we also have forgiven our debtors.
And lead us not into temptation,
but deliver us from evil." (Mt 6:9-13)

Try praying the Lord's prayer very slowly, pausing after each phrase to meditate on its meaning for you. The following is taken from a letter to Proba by St. Augustine, and it is worth contemplating his advice to help us pray the Lord's prayer with far more meaning and a lot less speed than we usually do:

We need to use words so that we may remind ourselves to consider carefully what we are asking, not so that we may think we can instruct the Lord or prevail on Him.

Thus, when we say: Hallowed be Your name, we are reminding ourselves to desire that His name, which in fact is always holy, should also be considered holy among men. I mean that it should not be held in contempt. But this is a help for men, not for God.

And as for our saying: Your kingdom come, it will surely come whether we will it or not. But we are stirring up our desires for the kingdom so that it can come to us and we can deserve to reign there.

When we say: Your will be done on earth as it is in heaven, we are asking Him to make us obedient so that His will may be done in us as it is done in heaven by His angels.

When we say: Give us this day our daily bread, in saying this day we mean "in this world." Here we ask for a sufficiency by specifying the most important part of it; that is, we use the word "bread" to stand for everything. Or else we are asking for the sacrament of the faithful, which is necessary in this world, not to gain temporal happiness but to gain the happiness that is everlasting.

When we say: Forgive us our trespasses as we forgive those who trespass against us, we are reminding ourselves of what we must ask and what we must do in order to be worthy in turn to receive.

When we say: Lead us not into temptation, we are reminding ourselves to ask that His help may not depart from us; otherwise we could be seduced and consent to some temptation, or despair and yield to it.

When we say: Deliver us from evil, we are reminding ourselves to reflect on the fact that we do not yet enjoy the state of blessedness in which we shall suffer no evil. This is the final petition contained in the Lord's Prayer, and it has a wide application. In this petition the Christian can utter his cries of sorrow, in it he can shed his tears, and through it he can begin, continue and conclude his prayer, whatever the distress in which he finds himself.[38]

The Holy Rosary

Catholic tradition holds that the Rosary was given to St. Dominic in a vision of the Blessed Virgin Mary, and Blessed Allan de la Roche then promoted it extensively. The practice of meditation during the praying of the Hail Marys was attributed to Dominic of Prussia, a 15th-century Carthusian monk, who called it the "Life of Jesus Rosary" (vita Christi Rosarium). The Christian victory at the Battle of Lepanto in 1571 was attributed to the praying of the Rosary by masses of Europeans based on the request of Pope Pius V. Eventually, it resulted in the Feast of Our Lady of the Rosary. In 1569, the papal bull Consueverunt Romani Pontifices established the devotion to the rosary in the Catholic Church. In 2002, St. John Paul II introduced the Luminous Mysteries, in addition to the existing three sets of mysteries, the Joyful, Sorrowful, and Glorious.

The Rosary is a meditation on the life of Jesus and Mary. When prayed slowly, meditatively, and with the heart, it is the best form of Christian meditation available to Catholics. Many Catholics are experimenting with forms of meditation that come from eastern religions in the hope of gaining centeredness of soul. I often wonder if they have ever tried praying the Rosary meditatively, for if they did so daily, there would be no need to dabble in other forms of meditation from other religions. The Church disagrees with syncretism, which is the attempt to integrate practices from other

---

[38] Saint Augustine, *Letters, Volume 2 (83–130) (The Fathers of the Church, Volume 18)* (CUA Press, 2010).

faiths into Catholicism. The Church has always been open to "synthesizing," which accepts what is good and wholesome in other cultures.

You should pray the Rosary by imagining that you are having an apparition of Our Lady right in the room where you are praying! Would you prattle off the Our Father and each Hail Mary without thinking about what the words mean and without saying them with heartfelt devotion? When you say the words "Hail Mary," you are essentially repeating the greeting that the angel Gabriel gave to Mary when he appeared to Her to announce the news that She was being asked to become the Mother of the Saviour. Think of how the angel would have said those words to Mary and then try saying them in a similar way when you pray the Rosary.

Next, when you announce each mystery and the meditation for it, place yourself in the actual scene of that mystery. If you are praying the first Joyful mystery, imagine yourself in Mary's small house and in the room where the angel Gabriel would have appeared to Her. Envision Mary's startled look and the angel's gentle reassurance to Her that God highly favours Her. Next, picture Mary's humble acceptance and submission to the angel's request on behalf of God when She finally responds: "Behold the handmaid of the Lord. Let what you have said be done unto me." Then pause for ten seconds before starting to pray the Our Father and the ten Hail Marys for that mystery. St. John Paul II recommended this ten-second pause in his book on how to pray the Rosary. Here is a good litmus test as to whether you are praying the Rosary meditatively: it should take you approximately half an hour to pray one set of mysteries (Joyful, Luminous, Sorrowful, or Glorious), and not fifteen minutes as is usually the case with most Catholics praying the Rosary.

The Key, The Door, and The Garden

In the 1990s, a priest from the Philippines frequently visited Toronto and various other cities in Canada, and his "healing" Masses were nothing short of miraculous. Many cures of both a spiritual and physical nature occurred at these Masses celebrated by this holy priest. I attended quite a few of his Masses, and I received a much-needed healing at one of his Masses in late 1999. I was experiencing a lot of anxiety regarding the many dire predictions being made about the year 2000. After Holy Communion, all the members of the congregation came forward one by one to be prayed over by this priest. As he laid his hands on my head and prayed, I felt a peace come over me that I had never felt in my life, and which has never left me since. A group of us once asked him how he prepared for his healing Masses. His response was simple but profound: he said that he prayed the full set of mysteries of the Rosary slowly and meditatively before each healing Mass. This undoubtedly took him at least two hours, but he was almost in a trance-like state when he came out of the sacristy for Mass. The holiness that radiated from him was noticeable to everyone in the congregation. Let that be a lesson for you and me!

The Road to Ceaseless Prayer

I would like to provide you with the analogy of an athlete beginning to train for a marathon. He starts by running one mile for the first week or two, then increases his distance slowly with each passing week, until six months later when he can finally run 26 miles. It is the same with your prayer life. If you start praying a few minutes a day for a week or two, then slowly increase the amount of time you pray, you might very well find yourself praying for two to three hours a day or more, which incidentally, Our Lady of Medjugorje has recommended that we should aim to achieve.

Do you simply want to exist in this world, or are you on a path of continual self-improvement? This is an important question to ask ourselves because it determines whether we are willing to take stock of our lives and honestly evaluate whether certain habits need to be changed. Repentance of the sins that we have committed in the past against the Lord and our neighbours is the first step on the journey to a new life. Then begins the life-long process of conversion based on "praying until prayer becomes a joy," and then "praying until prayer becomes your life!"

Begin now because every day that goes by is another day wasted, and conversion is a process that takes time and effort. If we have not become Saints before we die or before the Lord returns, then the best we can hope for is to make it to purgatory. But what if we do not make it to purgatory because we have unconfessed mortal sins on our souls, then the only place left for us to go is hell, and that is a real place of unceasing torment.

Summary

"Prayer is the raising of one's heart and mind to God or the requesting of good things from God." Most people, when they finish "praying," have not accomplished both the raising of their hearts *and* their minds to God or have not done so for a sufficiently long period to walk away being filled with God's grace, joy, and peace, and with the strength to face whatever their day is about to bring. Our Lady of Medjugorje has often stressed praying with the heart and not merely saying the words with your mind. Praying the Rosary with your heart, slowly and meditatively, is one of the best weapons we have in our journey to God. There is no such thing as standing still or remaining in the same place in the Christian life. You are either making progress and becoming holier, or you are sliding backward and becoming further removed from God and the Communion of Saints. Learn to pray and worship God in spirit and in truth, pray until prayer becomes a joy, and finally, pray until prayer becomes your life. Otherwise, you run the risk of losing your soul for all eternity.

17 A Model and Structure for Daily Prayer

In the chapter entitled "The Key," I discussed the importance, and I would almost say the necessity, of rising very early to welcome the Lord into your home and into your heart. The ideal time mentioned in that chapter was 3:00 AM, and I will assume that your schedule can allow you to pray until 5:00 AM, after which you can start preparation for your daily duties (family, work, etc.). You will undoubtedly have to work your way up to this schedule of early morning prayer. However, it can be achieved if you have the will to do it. Do not let technology rule you. You must rule technology and regain your quiet time. The rule of thumb mentioned in that chapter was to turn off all technology devices by 7:00 PM the night before, and that will give you plenty of time to get enough rest to wake up at 3:00 AM.

Here is an example of how your morning prayer can unfold from 3:00 AM to 5:00 AM:

- Begin your prayer time by making the sign of the cross and welcoming Jesus into your home and into your heart. Remember that all your prayers should be done by *lifting your heart and mind to God*. First allow a few minutes of silence as a sign of respect that God should be the One allowed to speak first in prayer.

- Next, say the regular morning offering prayer as follows: "O Jesus, through the Immaculate Heart of Mary, I offer you my prayers, works, joys, and sufferings of this day for all the intentions of your Sacred Heart, in union with the Holy Sacrifice of the Mass throughout the world, for the salvation of souls, the reparation of sins, the reunion of all Christians, and in particular for the intentions recommended by our Holy Father this month. Amen."

The Key, The Door, and The Garden

- Invoke the Holy Spirit to inspire your prayer time and to make it pleasing to the Lord. You can use the traditional Catholic invocation to the Holy Spirit as follows: "Come O Holy Spirit and fill the hearts of Thy faithful, and kindle in them the fire of Thy love. Send forth Thy Spirit, and they shall be created, and Thou shall renew the face of the earth. Let us pray. O God, who by the light of the Holy Spirit, instructs the hearts of Thy faithful, grant that by the same Spirit, we may be truly wise and ever rejoice in His consolation, through the same Christ, our Lord. Amen."

- You may want to consecrate your entire life to the Jesus Christ through the Immaculate Heart of Mary as this is highly recommended by the great Marian Saint, St. Louis De Montfort, and was practiced by many great Saints, such as the late St. John Paul II. You are essentially placing yourself under the protective mantle of Our Lady, and She will be sure to protect you and your family from all evil and lead you into the perfect will of the Father for your life.

- Next, you should invite Jesus to come and dwell within your heart for the entire day. A prayer for this was given in the chapter entitled "Make God the Centre of Your Life – Time is Short." I will repeat the prayer here: *"Jesus my Lord, my God, my King, my Saviour, my Good Shepherd, my Brother, my Friend, my Love, and my Everything, I know that you are standing right now at the door of my heart and knocking. I hear Your gentle voice, and I open wide the door of my heart to You. I humbly, sincerely, and lovingly invite You to come and dwell within me, for You are all that I desire in the land of the living. Come Lord Jesus and do not delay!"* This step is called the **INVITATION**.

A Model and Structure for Daily Prayer

- The next thing you will want to do is to give Jesus full permission to work within your soul whatever He wants to do. Ask Him to remove anything within you that is not of God and to mold you into His image. He needs your full permission to change you because He is humble and unassuming. He does not assume that because you have invited Him to dwell within you that He has your permission to change anything within you. This step is called the **PERMISSION**.

- Now that you have sincerely invited Jesus to dwell within you, and you have given Him full permission to act within your soul, you will want to completely submit yourself to the Father's will for your life that day and renew this every day. A simple prayer like the following will show your submission to the Father: "Heavenly Father, I humbly ask that Your most holy and divine will be accomplished in my life this day, for Your greater glory and for the good and salvation of my fellowman. Behold a servant of the Lord; let whatever You say be done unto me this day." This step is called the **SUBMISSION**.

- The next step is an important one as it is where you exchange burdens with the Lord. This technique was discussed in the chapter entitled "How to Stop Worrying for the Rest of Your Life." Essentially, you want to name all your burdens one by one and give them entirely to the Lord, without holding on to any of them. You should feel empty and peaceful when you have done this. Next, ask Jesus what specific burden He is carrying this morning that He would like you to help Him carry. Remain in silence and listen to His gentle voice. He may ask you to pray for the conversion of sinners, or families, or our youth. When you get a sense of what He wants you to pray for, spend the next five minutes or so and say, an Our Father, Hail Mary, and Glory Be for this burden of Jesus. Promise Him that all your prayers, works, and sufferings of that day will be for this burden of His. Remember, He will be taking care of your burdens, which you gave Him.

The above six steps should take you approximately half an hour, from 3:00 to 3:30 AM.

- Next, I strongly recommend the praying of the Liturgy of the Hours, which is the Church's universal prayer for priests and religious. Many laypeople around the world have joined in praying it, especially since Vatican II. You can use an online App for this, such as iBreviary or Universalis, but even better, you should purchase the book format and learn how to navigate the praying of the Liturgy of the Hours. I use and thoroughly enjoy the following book format: "Liturgy of the Hours (4-Volume Set) English Translation Prepared by the International Commission on English in the Liturgy Edition."

- From 3:30 to 4:00 AM, you should pray the following two components of the Liturgy of the Hours: (i) Office of Readings and (ii) Morning Prayer.

- From 4:00 to 4:30 AM, you can pray the particular mysteries of the Rosary for that day: Joyful on Mondays and Saturdays, the Luminous on Thursdays, the Sorrowful on Tuesdays and Fridays, and the Glorious on Wednesdays and Sundays.

- From 4:30 – 5:00 AM, you can read the Mass readings from the Bible for that day and then meditate on its meaning for your life.

A Model and Structure for Daily Prayer

- Finish by thanking God for your time of prayer and then make the sign of the Cross.

- An important point is necessary to make here: do not become proud when you are able to rise early and follow a prayer routine like the one shared above. That would be falling to a famous trap used by the devil on many a soul trying to make progress in the spiritual life through a solid prayer life. You should remember to say at least once a day, "I am a beggar and a sinner before God in prayer. I acknowledge that I do not know how to pray as I ought to."

Incidentally, I recommend praying the remainder of the Liturgy of the Hours during the day as each additional component takes only 5 minutes or so to complete. These include Mid-Morning Prayer (Terce) at 9:00 AM, Midday Prayer (Sext) at 12:00 PM, Mid-Afternoon Prayer (None) at 3:00 PM, Evening Prayer (Vespers) at 6:00 PM, and Night Prayer (Compline) at bedtime. You will then be praying with the Universal Church, and your prayer will have the power of millions of people around the world praying the same prayers at approximately the same time as you.

I also strongly recommend that you attend daily Mass and visit the Lord in the Blessed Sacrament in a Church or chapel near you. This forms part of Our Lady's "five stones" as discussed below and elsewhere in this book.

All the above prayers will take approximately three hours of your day, the same amount of time that you probably spend preparing and eating your meals. Your soul is more important than your body. Your body will decay one day but your soul will live forever, either in heaven or in hell. Do everything to ensure that your soul is strong and can win the spiritual battle that it is waging.

Invitation, Permission, and Submission

The three steps mentioned above, **Invitation, Permission,** and **Submission,** can be understood in terms of a master interior designer being invited into your home. If you only invited the designer into your home, that would be a pleasant first step because their company would be enjoyable. However, after the designer left, your home would be in the same condition as you left it, no better. You would not have benefitted from the expertise of the master interior designer. Jesus does not assume that because you have invited Him into your soul, that He has permission to act within you. He is very humble and waits for your express permission. Let us say that you go to the next step and grant the master interior designer full permission to clean up, remove, add any necessary furniture and accessories to your home, and even remodel the interior. You would now benefit from the expertise of your pleasant and talented guest. Thus far, you would have enjoyed remarkable company and have a more beautiful home. If you were to stop there and not give the keys of your home to the master interior designer, no one else might ever come to enjoy the beauty of your remodeled home, which would be a shame. If, however, you gave the keys to the designer with full submission to his will, then you will reap the fruit of many guests coming to your home who need the sanctuary of peace and healing now found in your home.

These are precisely the three steps that Our Lady demonstrated when She said "Yes" to the angel Gabriel's request to Her from God. By her constant prayerfulness, She was always inviting God to dwell within Her. When the angel waited for Her answer to God's request to conceive the Son of God in Her womb, She gave Her permission. And finally, She gave Her full submission to God's will for Her life when She said: "Behold, I am the servant of the Lord; let it be to me according to your word" (Lk 1:38). This was Her Fiat, and God awaits our fiat every day in prayer.

Do not be afraid to submit yourself completely to God's will because whatever He calls you to, He will give you the help you need to carry it out. Remember St. Paul's words: "I can do all things through Him who strengthens me" (Php 4:13).

Our Lady's Five Stones

I would like to quote Fr. Jozo Zovko, who was the parish priest of St. James when Our Lady allegedly started appearing to the six children in Medjugorje in 1981. He says:

> One lovely day in the history of Israel, the figure of Goliath came forth. He was a strong man, proud and invincible. Although Israel was incapable of imagining how it might defeat such a strong warrior, the Lord knew how to do it. He chose a young boy, a shepherd named David. The Lord told him to gather five stones in the river and face the giant. Trusting only in God's help, David went forth; he defeated and killed Goliath.
>
> Our Lady has chosen you, like David; you who are small, just as you are. She has suggested that you put five stones into your sack in order to overcome the atheism that surrounds us, that paganistic mentality that is being disseminated and seems invincible. Neither we nor the Church are capable of conquering materialism on our own. Our Lady has appeared in Medjugorje to declare that this is possible. Here are her five stones: Prayer,

Fasting, the Mass, the Bible and Confession. With these simple weapons we overcome the world.

I give you the weapons against your Goliath. Here are your little stones.

- Daily Prayer (especially the Rosary)
- Fasting on Wednesdays and Fridays on bread and water
- Daily Mass and Eucharist
- Monthly Confession
- Daily Reading of the Bible[39]

Spiritual Reading

One of the best ways to grow in your knowledge of the Catholic faith is to avail yourself of the many great books written by Saints and renowned Catholic writers. One book that comes to mind that helped me a lot as a layperson is "Introduction to the Devout Life" by St. Francis de Sales. It is the most famous Catholic self-help book of all time written for laypeople. This 17th-century book is a proven spiritual guide for living an authentic Christian life. There are other books with inspiring prayers and meditations, such as "The Imitation of Christ" by Thomas à Kempis. It is probably the most widely read Christian devotional work next to the Bible and is regarded as a devotional and religious classic. Another inspiring work is "The Story of a Soul," which is the autobiography of St. Thérèse of Lisieux. Here is a beautiful, simple but powerful quote from her book: "Our Lord does not look so much at the greatness of our actions, nor even at their difficulty, but at the love with which we do them."

---

[39] Fr. Jozo Zovko OFM, (Misma Notebooks, 1989).

A Model and Structure for Daily Prayer

Submitting to the Divine Will

An essential component in growing in holiness is your desire to submit entirely to the Divine Will of God for your life. Recall the solemn words of Jesus: "Not everyone who says to Me, 'Lord, Lord,' will enter the kingdom of heaven, but the one who does the will of My Father who is in heaven" (Mt 7:21). As we discussed above, an essential part of your morning prayer routine should be including a prayer like the following: "Heavenly Father, I pray that your most holy and divine will be accomplished in my life this day and all the remaining days of my life on earth, for Your greater glory and for the good and salvation of my fellowman. Father, behold a servant of the Lord; let whatever You say be done unto me this day." Once you have sincerely prayed that prayer, be attentive to the gentle promptings of the Holy Spirit throughout your day, and He will guide your actions and the events of your day to be in accordance with God's will for you that day. Do not try to force things in a particular direction if they are not falling into place in the way you want them to. Let the Spirit gently guide you in a new direction or to a different task if that is what He is prompting you to do. This will take time and maturity to master. Jesus and the Saints were masters at moving to the rhythm of the Spirit throughout all the hours and days of their lives. You and I can learn to become malleable in the hands of the Holy Spirit, and then each of our days will be ordered according to the will of God for our lives.

    A great work on living in the Divine Will can be found in the writings of the Catholic mystic Luisa Piccarreta (1865 – 1947), also known as the "Little Daughter of the Divine Will." She is being considered for possible canonization as a saint of the Catholic Church. Her spirituality centered on union with the Will of God.

The Key, The Door, and The Garden

Daniel O'Connor has written and commented extensively on Luisa Piccarreta's works. Two of his books are highly recommended to understand Luisa's writings as they were allegedly given to her by Jesus. These books are respectively: "The Crown of History"[40] and "The Crown of Sanctity."[41]

Summary

Here is a bold statement that I believe to be true and advisable to every Christian. You should aim for approximately three hours of formal prayer a day. This represents about 10% of the 24 hours in your day. It is like tithing your time to God, and He will surely bless and reward you for doing so. Our Lady of Medjugorje allegedly told the visionaries that we should be praying about three hours per day. Trust me that the Mother of God knows how to advise Her children to edify their spiritual lives!

Recall that in chapter 1 (God Exists, Guaranteed - From Atheist to Believer), I mentioned that some people do not feel particularly called to join one of the established orders or movements within the Catholic Church. These include the Third Order Franciscans, the Secular Franciscans, the lay Dominicans, the Opus Dei, the Society of the Little Flower of St. Thérèse of Lisieux, the Confraternity of Mary, Queen of all Hearts, and many more. You may want to adopt some aspects of the above orders and movements, which I do personally. You may simply be a layperson, married, or single who wants to take your faith seriously but struggle to do so. You may have

---

[40] Daniel O'Connor, *The Crown of History: The Imminent Glorious Era of Universal Peace* (Daniel O'Connor, 2019).

[41] Daniel O'Connor, *The Crown of Sanctity: On the Revelations of Jesus to Luisa Piccarreta* (Daniel O'Connor, 2019).

A Model and Structure for Daily Prayer

even gone one step further and embraced the vocation of a growing group of people within the Church called "dedicated singles", spoken of at length in her book "Single for a Greater Purpose"[42] by Luanne D. Zurlo. Then, the model and structure of prayer presented in this chapter (see the diagram below) will definitely help you stay in a loving and disciplined relationship with God. If, however, you are called to and already belong to one of the orders or movements mentioned above (or any of the others that exist), then you must try your best to stay faithful to the norms and practices of that order or movement. God has provided us with many ways to achieve and maintain our holiness within the Catholic Church, and we must remain faithful to them.

Finally, I would like to leave you with a diagram illustrating a simple model for your daily prayer life. It shows "The Key," which represents your rising very early before dawn to give the Lord the first place in your day before any of the noisy interruptions begin, which are so typical of modern living and which can sabotage your peace. The "five stones" of Our Lady are the five points of the star: daily Mass, daily Rosary, daily Scripture reading, weekly fasting, and monthly Confession. The praying of the Church's Liturgy of the Hours wraps itself around the whole day. Finally, all of your prayers must be done out of love for God. If you think that this will take too much time, I promise you that God will reward you for your love and dedication to Him by giving you the gift of divine time, and you will complete all of your daily activities in less time than you ordinarily would have taken to do them. Remember that God cannot be outdone in charity. Finally, the health of your soul is more important

---

[42] Luanne D. Zurlo, *Single for a Greater Purpose: A Hidden Joy in the Catholic Church* (Sophia Institute Press, 2019).

that the health of your body. Your body will decay one day but your soul will live forever, either in heaven or hell. Here is the diagram that can help you structure your prayer life:

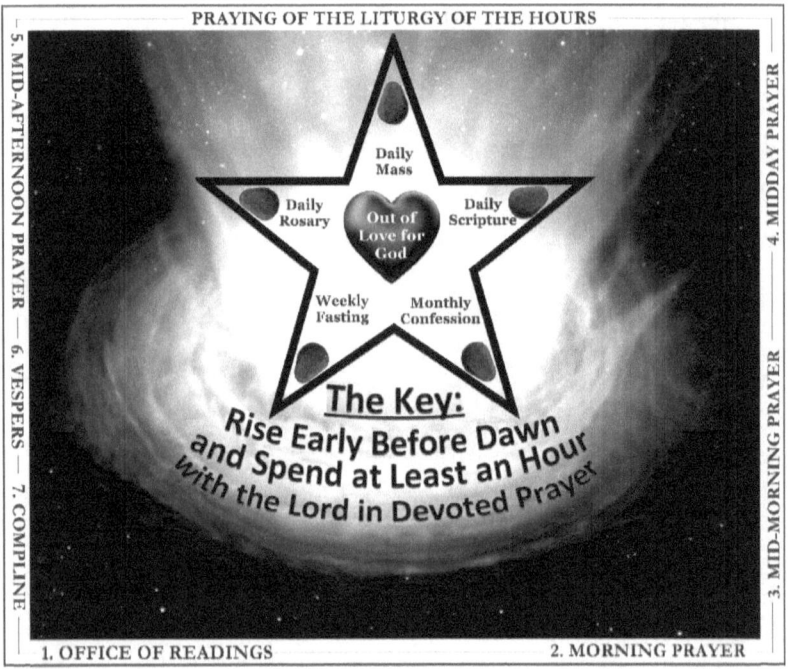

18 Not the Valley nor the Mountain, but the Plain

As we progress in our spiritual life, there are two pitfalls that we need to be very careful to avoid, and they are: (1) the sin of spiritual pride and (2) excessive sadness and self-pity. Both of these can easily lead us to fall into sin. In the first pitfall, we cause God to move away from us because He abhors pride. This represents our knowingly or unknowingly climbing the mountain of pride. In the second instance, we move away from God out of self-pity and isolation. God is to be found on the humble plain, but not on the mountain of pride nor in the valley of self-pity where we lack complete confidence in God's love for us.

Not on the Mountain: Avoiding the Sin of Spiritual Pride

Remember that there are many flavours and varieties of the sin of pride, and if the devil cannot get us with one type, he will try another until he succeeds. We have to be vigilant about the sin of spiritual pride because it is easy to fall into if we are not careful about the thoughts that roll around our minds as we make progress spiritually. We might find ourselves counting the number of spiritual activities we are involved in, and then look at others who are not doing as much as we are. We then mistakenly conclude that we are better than they are and that we are holier. A great antidote to this sin of spiritual pride is to honestly believe that you are always at the beginning of your spiritual journey, and that compared to the holiness of God and His wisdom, everyone's holiness and wisdom are about the same, almost zero. While celebrating Mass one day in 1273, St. Thomas Aquinas, the angelic Doctor of the Church, received a revelation from

God that caused him to stop writing, leaving his brilliant lifelong work, Summa Theologica, unfinished. He told his secretary: "The end of my labours has come. All I have written appears to be as so much straw after the things that have been revealed to me." When his friend begged him to finish writing, Thomas insisted: "I can write no more. I have seen things that make my writings like straw." The Saint died three months later.

St. Paul cautions us: "Therefore, let anyone who thinks that he stands take heed lest he fall" (1 Cor 10:12). The late theologian Charles John Ellicott commented on this simple but important line of Scripture as follows:

> This is the practical conclusion of the whole matter. We are to look back on that strange record of splendid privilege and of terrible fall and learn from it the solemn lesson of self-distrust. Led forth by divinely appointed leaders, overshadowed by the Divine Presence, supported by divinely given food and drink, the vast hosts of Israel had passed from the bondage of Egypt into the glorious liberty of children of the living God; yet amid all those who seemed to stand so secure in their relation to God, but a few fell not. Christians, called forth from a more deadly bondage into a more glorious liberty, are in like peril. Let the one who thinks that he stands secure take great heed, lest he fall. The murmuring against their apostolic teachers, the longing to go so far as they could in indulgence without committing actual sin, were terribly significant indications in the Corinthian Church. When we feel ourselves beginning to dislike those who warn us against sin, and when we find ourselves measuring with minute casuistry what is the smallest distance that we can place between ourselves and

some desired object of indulgence without actually sinning, then "let him that thinks he stands take heed lest he fall."[43]

We should also recall the parable that Jesus gave about the Pharisee and the tax collector standing in the temple: "Two men went up into the temple to pray, one a Pharisee and the other a tax collector. The Pharisee stood by himself and prayed this prayer: 'I thank you, God, that I am not like other people—cheaters, sinners, adulterers. I am certainly not like that tax collector! I fast twice a week; I give tithes of all that I get.' But the tax collector, standing far off, would not even lift up his eyes to heaven, but beat his breast, saying, 'God, be merciful to me, a sinner!'" (Lk 18:10-14). Alas, we often take the Pharisee's attitude and not that of the tax collector. If you find this happening to you ten times a day, then rebuke those thoughts and remember that one mortal sin will put you right back at square one, right at the beginning of your spiritual journey. God allows this to happen many times to us to save us from the sin of spiritual pride. He knows that the one sin that will definitely keep us out of heaven is pride, and He abhors it so much that He will remove His strength from us to allow us to fall, so that we quickly return to Him in a spirit of repentance and humility.

Remember that if you believe that you have committed a mortal sin (breaking one of the Ten Commandments with full knowledge and with full premeditated intent), then make a sincere act of contrition to God and try your best to confess that sin as soon as possible in the Sacrament of Confession. When we find ourselves in the Confessional confessing the same sin that we committed last month, how humbling that is for us, but what a remedy for our

---

[43] Charles John Ellicott, *Ellicott's Commentary for English Readers*.

spiritual pride. Learn from every fall because it can be seen as a call by God to move up higher in your relationship with Him. Whenever you find yourself falling into sin, no matter how hard you tried to resist the temptation, search diligently for how you have conducted yourself in your thoughts and actions recently. You will eventually detect one or more instances of pride in your life. Recall the line from the Book of Proverbs: "Pride goes before destruction, and a haughty spirit before a fall" (Prov 16:18). St. Paul also tells us that "No temptation has overtaken you that is not common to man. God is faithful, and he will not let you be tempted beyond your ability, but with the temptation he will also provide the way of escape, that you may be able to endure it. Therefore, my beloved, flee from idolatry" (1 Cor 10:13-14).

Let us also recall St. Paul cautioning the Romans (and all of Christendom by extension) not to think too highly of themselves because they believed in Christ, but that the Jews did not: "Then you will say, "Branches were broken off so that I might be grafted in." That is true. They were broken off because of their unbelief, but you stand fast through faith. *So do not become proud, but fear*" (Rom 11:19-20). We can often be like the Romans, thinking that we have made so much spiritual progress while other family members or our circle of friends have scarcely begun their journeys with Christ. We think of what will become of them if Christ were to return tomorrow because they are spiritually weak. Again, recall the parable which Jesus gave of the wage earners (Mt 20:1-16). The workers called at the eleventh hour to work (that is, 5:00 PM) were given the same wage as the workers who were called into the master's vineyard early in the morning. The first workers grumbled because they received the same salary as those called much later into the master's vineyard. We, too, must be careful in our thinking because a family member, friend, or even an enemy who has a "deathbed conversion" may end up in the same place or at an even higher position in heaven than us. God may judge that person less harshly than us, given their life's circumstances and setbacks that caused them to resist conversion until near death. On the other hand, God may see that we were given many graces early on in our lives and that we should have attained a much higher degree of sanctity than we achieved by the end of our lives. All of these should be sobering thoughts that help us avoid the sin of spiritual pride like the plague!

Humility is the foundation of all other virtues. Jesus said: "Whoever exalts himself will be humbled, and whoever humbles himself will be exalted" (Mt 23:12). Jesus also asked us to imitate Him: "Take my yoke upon you, and learn from me, for I am gentle and humble in heart, and you will find rest for your souls" (Mt 11:29). Are we gentle and humble of heart, or are we haughty and irritable with others? A great many Saints have commented that anger is a sure outward sign of inner pride. If you find yourself losing your patience often with others around you, even if they have given you valid reasons to do so, ask yourself if you are truly gentle and humble. Think of the many blows and insults that Jesus unjustly received during His twelve-hour long passion from Holy Thursday to Good Friday, and you will see that He did not have one angry outburst at his torturers and executioners. When He was finally nailed to the cross, the first words that came out of His mouth were: "Father, forgive them, for they know what they do" (Lk 23:24).

I have always found that the following advice given by Jesus to His disciples acts as a very humbling tool whenever I find myself thinking that I have achieved something worthwhile spiritually: "So you also, when you have done all that you were commanded, say, 'We are unworthy servants; we have only done what was our duty.'" (Lk

17:10). Can you imagine Jesus giving that advice to the men who went on to write the Gospels and the Letters of the New Testament, worked countless miracles, traveled on land by foot and abroad by sea, and were finally martyred or exiled? This was what they were supposed to say to themselves near the end of their lives. Where does that leave you and me? We cannot even say that we are unworthy servants! That leaves us with only one thing to say to the Lord when we reach the end of our lives: "Lord Jesus Christ, Son of God, have mercy on me, a sinner."

This is the One to Whom I Will Look

Finally, an excellent Scripture passage to give us a complete blueprint of humility and the attitude that God finds most pleasing in us is from Isaiah 66:2: "All these things my hand has made, and so all these things came to be, declares the LORD. But this is the one to whom I will look: he who is humble and contrite in spirit and trembles at my word."

If we are honest with ourselves, we are often not humble and contrite in spirit, and do we tremble at (i.e., awesomely respect) God's word. If we can strive to be in this state most of the time, then we will find it easier to take Jesus's advice: "Truly, I say to you, unless you turn and become like children, you will never enter the kingdom of heaven" (Mt 18:3). Sadly, the world teaches us the exact opposite. We are taught how to be independent and "self-made." Then, we wonder why we cannot seem to live the simple and humble life that Jesus asks us to live and which He Himself lived.

Not in the Valley: Avoiding Excessive Sadness and Self-pity

When we give into excessive sadness and self-pity, we are moving away from God into the valley while He stands gently and humbly on the plain, expecting us to do the same. It is worth recalling the original temptation used by Satan with Eve in the Garden of Eden. He made her believe that God did not want her and Adam to eat of the fruit of the tree of knowledge of good and evil because God was holding back something of His love from them. He essentially made Eve sad and melancholic, and in her weakened state, she fell prey to his temptation to eat of the forbidden fruit: "So when the woman saw that the tree was good for food, and that it was a delight to the eyes, and that the tree was to be desired to make one wise, she took of its fruit and ate, and she also gave some to her husband who was with her, and he ate" (Gen 3:6). This is a very common pattern that the evil one uses on us all, even to this very day. The next time you find yourself feeling melancholic and wallowing in self-pity, watch and see how quickly some temptation that you are usually weak against, comes readily to your mind and how often you give into that temptation, just like Eve did. Vigilance and astuteness are required here to not fall into the trap of the devil.

In his classic work on growing in holiness, St. Francis de Sales dedicates a whole chapter to this very problem:

> "The sorrow that is according to God," saith St. Paul, "worketh penance steadfast unto salvation; but the sorrow of the world worketh death." Therefore, sorrow may be either good or bad, according to its results upon us. Unfortunately, there are more bad than good results from it; for the good results are but two, namely,

mercy and repentance; whilst there are six evil results–anguish, indolence, indignation, jealousy, envy, and impatience; wherefore the Wise Man said, "Sadness hath killed many, and there is no profit in it" (Ecclus. 30:25), since from its source spring but two good and six evil rivers. It is only towards the good that the enemy employs sorrow as a temptation, for inasmuch as he seeks to make sinners take delight in their sin, so he seeks to make good works grievous to the good; and as he can only lead the one to evil by making it seem agreeable, so he can only deter the other from what is good by making it seem disagreeable. Satan delights in sadness and melancholy since he himself is sad and melancholy, and will be so to all eternity, a condition which he would have all to share with him.

Unholy sorrow disturbs the soul, disquiets her, arouses vain fears, disgusts her with prayer, overpowers the brain and makes it drowsy, deprives the soul of wisdom, resolution, judgment, and courage, and crushes her strength: in short, it resembles a hard winter, which withers the beauty of the earth and numbs all life, for it deprives the soul of all suppleness, rendering all her faculties of no avail and powerless.[44]

St. Francis de Sales goes on to provide some remedies when we see ourselves slipping into excessive sadness, melancholy, and self-pity:

If you are ever assailed by this hurtful sadness adopt the following remedies– "Is any among you sad?" asks St. James, "let him pray"

---

[44] Saint Francis de Sales, An *Introduction to the Devout Life* (TAN Books, 2010), 274-275.

(Jas 5:13). Prayer is a sovereign remedy, for it raises the soul to God, who is our only joy and consolation; but in prayer let your emotions and words, whether inward or outward, conduce to love and trust of God; such as, O God of pity, Merciful and Good God, Loving Saviour, God of my heart, my Joy, my Hope, my Beloved Spouse, Beloved of my soul, and such as these.[45]

But in the Plain: Meet God on Level Ground

The valley we have spoken about above (i.e., excessive sadness, melancholy, and self-pity) is an unstable downward slope that leads us away from God into the darkness of self-isolation. The mountain we referred to above (i.e., pride and above all, spiritual pride) is an upward slope that leads God away from us because He abhors pride. Psalm 23 should remind us of the level plain where we are at peace with God and enjoy His company: "The LORD is my shepherd; I shall not want. He makes me lie down in green pastures. He leads me beside still waters. He restores my soul. He leads me in paths of righteousness for his name's sake" (Ps 23:1-3).

Excesses are usually never good in life, and that is why the excess of the valley and the excess of the mountain do not bode well for a long-standing, loving relationship with God. The level plain is stable and peaceful. We should do regular internal checks in our soul to see if we are residing there or sliding downwards into the isolating valley of sadness or ascending the arrogant slope of pride. Here is how you can tell: sin will accompany either of these two extremes. Holiness and peace with God usually accompany our residing on the level plain with God.

---

[45] Ibid, 275.

Summary

Not in the valley nor on the mountain is God usually found, but on the humble plain where He wants to meet you and have a loving relationship with you. Do not think you are standing lest you fall. Shun spiritual pride and all other forms of pride and imitate your Master. Humility is the foundation of all other virtues. Do not compare yourself to others and think that you are better than them. Always remember that you are only one mortal sin away from going right back to the beginning of your Christian journey. In the case of mortal sin, Sacramental Confession is needed to reintegrate you into the full sacramental life of the Church. Then a reflection on your interior state prior to your fall will indicate the type of pride you succumbed to. Resolve to avoid that type of pride at all costs.

Finally, remember that we are even less than unworthy servants in the eyes of the Lord, but still very much loved by Him. Also, avoid excessive sadness and self-pity because that is an age-old ploy of the devil that he used on Eve to get her to eat the forbidden fruit. He tries the same tactic with us today and succeeds quite often. Try as much as possible to reside peacefully with God on the level plain of holiness, and you will find that sin has little power over you.

19 Persevere, Persevere, Persevere!

We have discussed many truths and methods in the three sections of this book, The Call, The Foundation, and The Response. But all of them will be of little or no use to you if you do not persevere on your Christian journey through this valley of tears (a line from the Hail Holy Queen prayer). O how tempting it sometimes is to simply throw in the towel and say to yourself that this Christian journey of ups and downs is too difficult, and that what Jesus asks of us is nearly impossible to accomplish. After all, He did say: "You therefore must be perfect, as your heavenly Father is perfect" (Mt 5:48). But who can realistically achieve perfection? It is our lifelong of striving to be perfect in loving God and loving our neighbour that God honours in our spiritual journey. Jesus' words are sobering: "But the one who endures to the end will be saved" (Mt 24:13). This means that if we do not persevere until the end, we will not be saved. Suppose Jesus had said to His Father in the Garden of Gethsemane that His impending crucifixion and subsequent rejection by so many men and women in the future was too difficult to endure, and that He was simply going to disappear back into heaven. Where would that have left us? It would have left us without the sacrifice that has saved countless souls throughout the ages.

Similarly, when most of His Apostles were faced with martyrdom (all but John were martyred), if they had denied Jesus to save their own lives, they would not have made it to heaven. You can read in some of the traditions of the Church how gruesome were the Apostles' martyrdom! Thus, when you find yourself facing some challenging trial or period in your life, say to yourself that, at least this trial is not as painful as being flayed alive (St. Bartholomew), or crucified upside down (St. Peter), or being staked to the earth by spears and then beheaded (St. Matthew). I think you get my point!

The Catechism of the Catholic Church provides us with insight and comfort in our struggles with sin and trying to achieve Christian perfection:

> The consequences of original sin and of all men's personal sins put the world as a whole in the sinful condition aptly described in St. John's expression, "the sin of the world." This expression can also refer to the negative influence exerted on people by communal situations and social structures that are the fruit of men's sins.
>
> This dramatic situation of "the whole world [which] is in the power of the evil one" makes man's life a battle:
>
> The whole of man's history has been the story of dour combat with the powers of evil, stretching, so our Lord tells us, from the very dawn of history until the last day. Finding himself in the midst of the battlefield man has to struggle to do what is right, and it is at great cost to himself, and aided by God's grace, that he succeeds in achieving his own inner integrity.[46]

There are great rewards to be reaped when we persevere through heart-breaking trials in our lives. How often we give up just before God is about to send us relief and even a surprise turn of events along with His consolation. The following excerpt is taken from a homily on the Gospels by St. Gregory the Great, pope:

When Mary Magdalene came to the tomb and did not find the Lord's body, she thought it had been taken away and so informed

---

[46] *Catechism of the Catholic Church, Second Edition* (Libreria Editrice Vaticana, 1994, 1997), no. 408-409.

the disciples. After they came and saw the tomb, they too believed what Mary had told them. The text then says: The disciples went back home, and it adds: but Mary wept and remained standing outside the tomb.

We should reflect on Mary's attitude and the great love she felt for Christ; for though the disciples had left the tomb, she remained. She was still seeking the one she had not found, and while she sought, she wept; burning with the fire of love, she longed for him who she thought had been taken away. And so it happened that the woman who stayed behind to seek Christ was the only one to see him. For perseverance is essential to any good deed, as the voice of truth tells us: Whoever perseveres to the end will be saved.

At first, she sought but did not find, but when she persevered it happened that she found what she was looking for. When our desires are not satisfied, they grow stronger, and becoming stronger they take hold of their object. Holy desires likewise grow with anticipation, and if they do not grow, they are not really desires. Anyone who succeeds in attaining the truth has burned with such a great love. As David says: My soul has thirsted for the living God; when shall I come and appear before the face of God? And so also in the Song of Songs the Church says: I was wounded by love; and again: My soul is melted with love.[47]

From the above reflection on St. Mary Magdalene, we see that our perseverance is a sign of our love for God. Similarly, our lack of endurance indicates that our love for God is shallow at best, or even

---

[47] St. Gregory the Great, pope, *She longed for Christ, though she thought He had been taken away* (Homily 25, 1-2, 4-5:PL 76, 1189-1193).

worse, non-existent! If we persevere in the trials of marriage and raising children, we do so because we love our spouse and children. How many grievous trials and setbacks husbands and wives experience in their earthly lives, and yet they are called to persevere through these trials. Similarly, priests and religious often experience long periods of suffering and are nevertheless called to persevere in their vocations. How about the sufferings we experience in our jobs and in the workplace? These are many and varied, but if we give up and do not persevere, we are likely to find ourselves unemployed and unable to provide for our families. If we have learned the benefits of persevering in the temporal affairs of our lives where the stakes are earthly, why are we so easily tempted to give up when our spiritual trials seem unbearable? In this latter case, the stakes are eternal, and so all the more reason why we should persevere.

The Dark Night of the Soul – Who Moved?

You may be familiar with St. John of the Cross's "Dark Night of the Soul," where God tests the soul by removing almost all consolation in prayer. You practically cannot feel God's presence in your life, and when you pray, there is nothing but dryness. You feel as though God is a million miles away and not even listening to your prayers. This dryness happens to some people as they become very spiritually advanced. God now desires to test whether they love Him because of the consolations and blessings that He has given them through prayer or whether they love Him for who He is in Himself.

I want to relate a story to you to distinguish whether you might be going through the "dark night of the soul" or whether something else might be happening in your prayer life. In the late 1990s, I attended a Mass at St. Rose of Lima parish in Toronto, Canada, with some friends on the Sunday after Easter Sunday (the Feast of Divine Mercy). A Jesuit priest who was quite advanced in age gave a powerful sermon about this very same issue of dryness in prayer. He said that he was often approached by parishioners who were experiencing this dryness to determine if they were going through the "dark night of the soul." I will never forget what he said in his homily, so etched it is in my mind: "If you once felt yourself close to God and now you no longer do, ask yourself one question: who moved?" Essentially, he meant that we could easily slip in our prayer life and our relationship with God because we have become too busy with the chores of life and have consciously or unconsciously become neglectful of our spiritual life. We are then too quick to assume that God is testing us by allowing us to feel this dryness. The reality is that God never moved away from us; it is we who have moved away from God! Thus, before you feel like giving up because your relationship with God seems dry, make an honest evaluation of the time since you last felt close to God and determine if you have slipped in your quality and quantity of prayer. If you have, make a gentle but firm commitment to return to your former relationship with God. This is another weapon in persevering on your spiritual journey.

To Rejoice is the Reap Joy by Choice

There are times on our Christian journey through this challenging life when we are tempted to give up because our trials are so many and sustained. A great weapon to use in times like these is to praise God in hymns and songs of praise. I know that it is difficult to do so, but if you make an act of your will and just praise God, He will reward you by lightening your burdens. I like to say that "to rejoice is to reap joy by choice." St. Paul advises us: "Rejoice in the Lord always. Again

I will say, rejoice" (Phil 4:4). "Rejoice in hope, be patient in tribulation, be constant in prayer" (Rom 12:12).

We read in Psalm 33: "Shout for joy in the LORD, O you righteous! Praise befits the upright. Give thanks to the LORD with the lyre; make melody to him with the harp of ten strings! Sing to him a new song; play skillfully on the strings, with loud shouts" (Ps 33:1-3).

The prophet Habakkuk composed his book under God's motivation to caution Judah that God was going to utilize a foreign country to punish Israel due to her infidelities. Even though Habakkuk was scared at the coming judgment, he accepted that he could pick how he would react to whatever came. He could either surrender to sadness or celebrate God's liberating power. He chose the latter: "Though the fig tree should not blossom, nor fruit be on the vines, the produce of the olive fail and the fields yield no food, the flock be cut off from the fold and there be no herd in the stalls, yet I will rejoice in the LORD; I will take joy in the God of my salvation. GOD, the Lord, is my strength; he makes my feet like the deer's; he makes me tread on my high places" (Hab 3:17-19).

Let us also recall the story of how Paul and Silas chose to react when they were beaten with rods and put in prison. We too are often "beaten up" by life and other people and placed in symbolic prisons:

> The crowd joined in attacking them, and the magistrates tore the garments off them and gave orders to beat them with rods. And when they had inflicted many blows upon them, they threw them into prison, ordering the jailer to keep them safely. Having received this order, he put them into the inner prison and fastened their feet in the stocks.

Persevere, Persevere, Persevere!

About midnight Paul and Silas were praying and singing hymns to God, and the prisoners were listening to them, and suddenly there was a great earthquake, so that the foundations of the prison were shaken. And immediately all the doors were opened, and everyone's bonds were unfastened. When the jailer woke and saw that the prison doors were open, he drew his sword and was about to kill himself, supposing that the prisoners had escaped. But Paul cried with a loud voice, "Do not harm yourself, for we are all here." And the jailer called for lights and rushed in, and trembling with fear he fell down before Paul and Silas. Then he brought them out and said, "Sirs, what must I do to be saved?" And they said, "Believe in the Lord Jesus, and you will be saved, you and your household." And they spoke the word of the Lord to him and to all who were in his house. And he took them the same hour of the night and washed their wounds; and he was baptized at once, he and all his family. Then he brought them up into his house and set food before them. And he rejoiced along with his entire household that he had believed in God. (Acts 16:22-34).

We thus see from the above Scripture passages that a great weapon to help us in persevering through times of trial is to praise God regardless of how we are feeling. Learn some hymns and songs of praise by heart and sing them often to lift your spirit and encourage yourself.

The Key, The Door, and The Garden

Will You Laugh at Me or Will You Wipe My Face?

I have been called to climb a mountain that is difficult and steep,
And the obstacles along the way can be unexpected and deep.
Then I reach a plateau and take some rest,
Only to be called up higher to achieve my best.

I begin the climb again to a higher plateau,
Against the wishes of my soul's long-time foe.
Berated, belittled, and left all alone,
I sigh and breathe deeply as I hear my soul moan!

At times, the climb is so hard that I fall far below
The plateau I just left to see my soul grow.
Despondent and wounded, I start over again,
As my determination builds to what it was back then.

To the world, I must seem delusional or maybe too driven,
But I will not rest until I have fully striven.
To reach what or where you may ask?
My true home is what my Saviour has set as my task.

So, if you see me with clothes tattered and torn,
With my face covered in sweat and blood, looking forlorn,
Will you laugh at me, or will you wipe my face?
Remember what that brave woman did to gain the Saviour's grace!

Our paths may cross briefly here and there,
As it did with the Saviour and that woman without fear.
Oh yes, the crowds mocked Him and laughed as He passed by,
Will you laugh at me, or will you wipe my face when I sigh?

Anthony Hadeed
9 September 2018

Summary

On our Christian journey, unless we persevere until the end, we will not be saved. Jesus and His Apostles, as well as many of the early Christian martyrs, died for their faith. The 20th century has seen more Christian martyrs than all of the other centuries combined. They courageously persevered until the end. Our Christian journey is marked by many ups and downs, and our perseverance through them all will indicate our sincere love for God.

We persevere in our earthly trials, for which the stakes are mostly temporal, so how much more should we persevere in our spiritual life where the stakes are eternal. If we find ourselves in times of dryness in prayer, before assuming that God is putting us through the "dark night of the soul," ask yourself one question: who moved? Finally, amid trials, you can choose to rejoice and sing hymns and songs of praise to God because to rejoice is to reap joy by choice. Joy will come over you that will help you persevere in these times of trial.

20 Seek Fellowship with Other Christians

There is a familiar saying: There is no such thing as a lone ranger Christian. We have often heard many family members and friends say that they do not need to go to Church because they pray to God in the privacy of their homes. Most certainly, we are called by Jesus to pray to God in secret: "But when you pray, go into your room and shut the door and pray to your Father who is in secret. And your Father who sees in secret will reward you" (Mt 6:6). This is the private component of our prayer life, which has been discussed in many of this book's chapters. However, there is another dimension to our spirituality and Christian prayer: the believing and praying Christian community.

Here is sound advice from the Letter to the Hebrews: "And let us consider how to stir up one another to love and good works, not neglecting to meet together, as is the habit of some, but encouraging one another, and all the more as you see the Day drawing near" (Heb 10:24-25). It is a sign of self-reliant pride and possibly sloth when someone decides to stay away from the believing body of Christ and pursue their own brand of spirituality.

Jesus gave us a tremendous promise when He said: "Again I say to you, if two of you agree on earth about anything they ask, it will be done for them by my Father in heaven. For where two or three are gathered in my name, there am I among them" (Mt 18:19-20). The most obvious place of fellowship, which is accompanied by the most powerful prayer on earth, is the Holy Sacrifice of the Mass. All Catholic Christians are obliged to participate in Mass once for the weekend, either on the vigil on Saturday evening or anytime on Sunday according to the schedule of your local parish. Please take the following teaching of the Church seriously because it has become so neglected in our time. If a Catholic Christian willingly and knowingly misses attending Holy Mass on a given weekend without any valid reason (emergency, illness of oneself, or a family member in your care), this constitutes grave sin. This sin must be confessed in the Sacrament of Reconciliation before receiving the Eucharist at your next Mass. Sadly, there is such abuse in this regard in modern times; people miss attending Mass for no valid reason for months or even years at a time but then attend a funeral, wedding, Easter Mass, or Christmas Mass. They then proceed to receive Holy Communion without the slightest thought of Confession. Remember that receiving Holy Communion in the state of mortal sin does you no good and is even harmful to your soul.

In addition to participating in Holy Mass once for the weekend, many Catholic Christians feel called to attend Mass daily and receive the Eucharist. This is a wonderful calling and grace, and one that further enriches and strengthens your soul, both from receiving Jesus' Body, Blood, Soul, and Divinity so often, and from hearing the Word of God every day and meditating on its meaning in your life.

Many Christians are also called to join prayer groups where the Rosary is prayed, intercession is made for local and global causes, or the Bible is studied as a group. These are beautiful additions to one's spirituality, and they decrease the sense of isolation that many Christians feel. Another advantage of these prayer groups is their smallness and intimacy, which can be very encouraging, especially in times of trials and hardships.

The Catechism of the Catholic Church also speaks of secular institutes and societies of apostolic life among the laity. These are more official gatherings of Catholic Christians that serve particular purposes for society:

Secular institutes

"A secular institute is an institute of consecrated life in which the Christian faithful living in the world strive for the perfection of charity and work for the sanctification of the world especially from within." By a "life perfectly and entirely consecrated to [such] sanctification," the members of these institutes share in the Church's task of evangelization, "in the world and from within the world," where their presence acts as "leaven in the world." "Their witness of a Christian life" aims "to order temporal things according to God and inform the world with the power of the gospel." They commit themselves to the evangelical counsels by sacred bonds and observe among themselves the communion and fellowship appropriate to their "particular secular way of life."

Societies of apostolic life

Alongside the different forms of consecrated life are "societies of apostolic life whose members without religious vows pursue the particular apostolic purpose of their society, and lead a life as brothers or sisters in common according to a particular manner of life, strive for the perfection of charity through the observance of the constitutions. Among these there are societies in which the members embrace the evangelical counsels" according to their constitutions.

Finally, some people are called to belong to lay orders or movements within the Church, such as the Third Order Franciscans, Secular Franciscans, the lay Dominicans, the Opus Dei, the Society of the Little Flower of St. Thérèse of Lisieux, the Confraternity of

Mary, Queen of all Hearts, to name a few. The charisms of certain lay orders and movements appeal to different people depending on their personalities and inner calling. I know many people who like the structure and order (i.e., "norms") that characterize the Opus Dei, along with the associated scheduled fellowship meetings. I also know people who have taken the vows of third-order Dominicans because the spirituality of St. Dominic appeals to them. I have always felt personally drawn to St. Francis of Assisi's spirituality and his love for poverty and all of God's creatures. I also practice daily St. Thérèse's "Little Way," and of course, the "five stones" recommended by Our Lady of Medjugorje.

Summary

There is no such thing as a lone ranger Christian. Participation at Sunday Mass is a weekly obligation (and joy) for all Catholic Christians. We need the fellowship of other Christians; otherwise, we risk turning inward and developing our own erroneous beliefs about Jesus and His Church. Participation in daily Mass is a great call and privilege that is available to everyone. Seeking additional fellowship with other like-minded Christians in prayer groups, secular institutes, societies of apostolic life, and other lay "orders" within the Church can be very beneficial to our spiritual growth. It can build strength, conviction and alleviate loneliness and isolation.

21 Be a Part of the New Evangelization

In his encyclical "Redemptoris Missio," St. John Paul II stated: "I wish to invite the Church to renew her missionary commitment. The present document has as its goal an interior renewal of faith and Christian life. For missionary activity renews the Church, revitalizes faith and Christian identity, and offers fresh enthusiasm and new incentive. Faith is strengthened when it is given to others! It is in commitment to the Church's universal mission that the new evangelization of Christian peoples will find inspiration and support."[48]

Further on in the same document, he makes his call to the new evangelization clear: "God is opening before the Church the horizons of a humanity more fully prepared for the sowing of the Gospel. I sense that the moment has come to commit all of the Church's energies to a new evangelization and to the mission ad gentes (to the Gentiles). No believer in Christ, no institution of the Church can avoid this supreme duty: to proclaim Christ to all peoples."[49]

St. John Paul II goes so far as saying that many people in traditionally Christian countries have practically lost their faith. We discussed some of the reasons for this in the chapter of this book entitled "A Spiritual Pandemic Affecting the Whole World," and in particular, in the section "Idolatry Abounds Everywhere." Recall in the same chapter that we reviewed a term used in modern theology called "practical atheism" or "fluid atheism." This is spoken of at length in the book by Robert Cardinal Sarah, entitled "The Day Is

---

[48] St. John Paul II, pope *Redemptoris Missio: Encyclical Letter on the Permanent Validity of the Church's Missionary Mandate* (7 December 1990).
[49] Ibid.

The Key, The Door, and The Garden

Now Far Spent." He believes that the common root of all current crises is found in this fluid atheism, which, without denying God, lives in practice as if He did not exist. "I think that our time is experiencing the temptation to atheism. Not the hard, militant atheism we have seen aping Christianity through Marxist or Nazi pseudo-liturgies. That sort of atheism, a kind of religion in reverse, has become discreet. I mean, rather, a subtle, dangerous state of mind: fluid atheism. Now that is an insidious, dangerous sickness, even though its first symptoms seem benign...We must realize that this fluid atheism runs through our veins. It never stays the same, but it infiltrates everywhere."[50]

St. John Paul II stated in the same encyclical quoted above: "Thirdly, there is an intermediate situation, particularly in countries with ancient Christian roots, and occasionally in the younger Churches as well, where entire groups of the baptized have lost a living sense of the faith, or even no longer consider themselves members of the Church, and live a life far removed from Christ and his Gospel. In this case what is needed is a "new evangelization" or a "re-evangelization.""[51]

It has become evident to many faithful Catholics and Christians of other denominations that God is calling His loyal followers to become disciples of the "last times." When I use the phrase "last times," it may evoke the apocalypse in some readers. In others, it may also elicit the times of the Great Tribulation predicted by Jesus in Matthew's Gospel, chapter 24. In either case, it is hard to deny that

---

[50] Robert Cardinal Sarah, Nicolas Diat, *The Day Is Now Far Spent* (Ignatius Press, 2019), 334-335.

[51] St. John Paul II, pope, *Redemptoris Missio: Encyclical Letter on the Permanent Validity of the Church's Missionary Mandate* (7 December 1990).

our world has returned to almost paganism but with a sophisticated and technological twist, which makes it even more dangerous than the original paganism, which Jesus came to eradicate.

Many Saints and theologians have predicted that near the end time, God will raise up people whose holiness will be unparalleled in history and that they will be given the express mission of evangelizing and re-evangelizing the world before Jesus Christ's return. In particular, St. Louis Marie de Montfort wrote about this very fact in 1712 in his book "True Devotion to Mary":

"I said that this will happen especially towards the end of the world, and indeed soon, because Almighty God and his holy Mother are to raise up great saints who will surpass in holiness most other saints as much as the cedars of Lebanon tower above little shrubs. This has been revealed to a holy soul whose life has been written by M. de Renty. These great souls filled with grace and zeal will be chosen to oppose the enemies of God who are raging on all sides. They will be exceptionally devoted to the Blessed Virgin. Illumined by her light, strengthened by her food, guided by her spirit, supported by her arm, sheltered under her protection, they will fight with one hand and build with the other. With one hand they will give battle, overthrowing and crushing heretics and their heresies, schismatics and their schisms, idolaters and their idolatries, sinners, and their wickedness. With the other hand they will build the temple of the true Solomon and the mystical city of God, namely, the Blessed Virgin, who is called by the Fathers of the Church the Temple of Solomon and the City of God. By word and example, they will draw all men to a true devotion to her and though this will make many enemies, it will also bring about many victories and much glory to God alone.

The Key, The Door, and The Garden

This is what God revealed to St. Vincent Ferrer, that outstanding apostle of his day, as he has amply shown in one of his works."[52]

Now, where do all of these predictions and calls to the new evangelization leave us? It leaves us with two choices. We can accept the challenge, grow in holiness, and do God's will in leading many souls back to God before it is too late. Conversely, we ignore the call and leave it to others to carry out perhaps the most significant work ever called for by the Almighty before He brings the world to an end. It will give us great comfort to learn from the early days of the Church when the Apostles and disciples of Jesus were called to witness to Jesus' teachings, His death, and His resurrection to the Jews and the pagan nations. The first 350 years of Christianity saw countless martyrs until Emperor Constantine made Christianity the Roman Empire's official religion. Some of these accounts of the early Christian evangelists can be found in Sacred Scripture in the Acts of the Apostles. If you consider the many countries that St. Paul, the greatest evangelist the Church has ever known, brought the Gospel to, when there were no cars, planes, or other easy means of transportation, it puts us all to shame. Consider also how many letters he wrote to the early Christian communities he had helped to form, all when writing a simple page of text without mistakes was reserved to specialized scribes. If he had access to our modern means of transportation and writing (such as computers and publishing companies), he might very well have evangelized the whole world single-handedly!

---

[52] Saint Louis de Montfort, Reverend Frederick William Faber, D.D., *True Devotion to Mary* (Lulu.com, 2014).

Be a Part of the New Evangelization

The call to be a part of the new evangelization begins with consecrating yourself entirely to the Immaculate Heart of Mary, as St. Louis De Montfort strongly recommended in his famous book "True Devotion to Mary." St. John Paul II said that this was the single most profound book that changed his entire life! Can you imagine those riveting words from such a great Saint in modern times? So profound was that book in influencing St. John Paul II's spirituality that he made the motto of his papacy "Totus Tuus," which translated into English means "Totally yours," referring to his complete devotion to Mary. Who can deny the abundant fruit that the life of St. John Paull II yielded for Christ and His Church! He made 129 visits to various countries during his pontificate, and additionally, he made 146 pastoral visits to Italy. He wrote 14 Papal encyclicals during his 26-year pontificate and was credited with assisting with the fall of Communism in Russia and Eastern Europe. I think that you and I should look a lot more closely at his motto "Totus Tuus" and make it our own.

St. Louis De Montfort lays out a series of prayers and meditations in his book, coupled with the Rosary that lasts for 33 days, which set a person's life on the path of total consecration to the Immaculate Heart of Mary. Jesus spent his entire 30 years in Nazareth under Mary's watchful care. She was also present silently and sometimes publicly during His three years of ministry, and finally at the foot of the cross when He was crucified. If this was the example that Jesus left for us, it is incredible that some Christians believe that they can accomplish God's will and get to heaven without the slightest devotion to Mary. This attitude amounts to placing oneself and one's wisdom above that of Jesus – not highly recommended!

A very important beatitude that you need to possess to be a part of the new evangelization is poverty of spirit. You need to shed all unnecessary material possessions and live as simply as possible. This refers to your place of abode, your clothes, your means of transportation, your food, and so on. You might ask why this is a necessary step to be an effective instrument in the Lord's hands for the new evangelization. The answer is simple: the first beatitude that Jesus taught us was, "Blessed are the poor in spirit, theirs is the kingdom of heaven" (Mt 5:3). Jesus goes on to list the other seven beatitudes, but the foundational one is poverty of spirit. Having too many material possessions weighs us down and makes us unfruitful. Recall the parable of the sower: "And as for what fell among the thorns, they are those who hear, but as they go on their way they are choked by the cares and riches and pleasures of life, and their fruit does not mature" (Lk 8:14).

Another essential virtue to possess for participating in the new evangelization is the virtue of chastity. The only people who can engage in sexual activity without sinning are validly married couples. Every other person on the planet should be living celibately. Even though this may sound harsh and hard to live by, it is the truth as taught by the Catholic Church. The purpose of the conjugal act is to foster unity and fecundity between a married couple. The use of the sexual faculty for any other reason and by any other human being has negative consequences, as time eventually reveals. If you are not involved in a valid marriage in the eyes of the Church, then to live celibately, you need to pray daily for this grace from God. Tell Him of your struggles in this area and ask Him to give you the strength and even the joy to live celibately. Likewise, the consequences will be positive and fruitful, and God can use you mightily in the new evangelization of the world. Remember as well that human marriage does not exist in heaven as Jesus confirmed to the Sadducees who doubted the resurrection: "For in the resurrection they neither marry nor are given in marriage, but are like angels in heaven" (Mt 22:30).

The last vital virtue of being part of the new evangelization is that of obedience. Complete obedience to the Magisterium of the Church and its teachings is crucial to spread the truth about Jesus Christ. St. Augustine of Hippo was one of the first people to call himself a Catholic Christian, which meant a person who believed and upheld everything that the universal Church of Rome taught. This was to distinguish himself and fellow Catholic Christians down through the ages from other Christians who were following partially erroneous teachings and beliefs. Make sure you own a copy of the Catechism of the Catholic Church and the Holy Bible and that you refer to them often for your education in proper Catholic doctrine on faith and morals.

The above three virtues discussed are called the evangelical counsels: poverty, chastity, and obedience. While these three counsels are professed in an explicit and public way by disciples of Christ vowed to the religious life, they can be practiced to varying degrees by laypeople who have discerned a call to be a part of the new evangelization. We read in the Catechism:

> Christ proposes the evangelical counsels, in their great variety, to every disciple. The perfection of charity, to which all the faithful are called, entails for those who freely follow the call to consecrated life the obligation of practicing chastity in celibacy for the sake of the Kingdom, poverty and obedience. It is the profession of these counsels, within a permanent state of life

recognized by the Church, that characterizes the life consecrated to God.[53]

The First Evangelization as a Model for the New Evangelization

In his Apostolic Letter, "Novo Millennio Ineunte," St. John Paul II stated clearly what the New evangelization should look like:

> Even in countries evangelized many centuries ago, the reality of a "Christian society" which, amid all the frailties which have always marked human life, measured itself explicitly on Gospel values, is now gone. Today we must courageously face a situation which is becoming increasingly diversified and demanding, in the context of "globalization" and of the consequent new and uncertain mingling of peoples and cultures. Over the years, I have often repeated the summons to the new evangelization. I do so again now, especially in order to insist that we must rekindle in ourselves the impetus of the beginnings and allow ourselves to be filled with the ardour of the apostolic preaching which followed Pentecost. We must revive in ourselves the burning conviction of Paul, who cried out: "Woe to me if I do not preach the Gospel" (1 Cor 9:16)."[54]

Here is what the first evangelization looked like in the early days of the Apostles, and what it must look like in the new evangelization:

---

[53] *Catechism of the Catholic Church, Second Edition* (Libreria Editrice Vaticana, 1994, 1997), no. 915.

[54] St. John Paul II, pope, *Apostolic Letter, Novo Millennio Ineunte* (6 January 2001)

Be a Part of the New Evangelization

"And more than ever believers were added to the Lord, multitudes of both men and women so that they even carried out the sick into the streets and laid them on cots and mats, that as Peter came by, at least his shadow might fall on some of them. The people also gathered from the towns around Jerusalem, bringing the sick and those afflicted with unclean spirits, and they were all healed" (Acts 5:14-16). Again, we read in the Acts of the Apostles how St. Paul worked many miracles himself in addition to St. Peter and the other Apostles and disciples of the early Church. "And God was doing extraordinary miracles by the hands of Paul, so that even handkerchiefs or aprons that had touched his skin were carried away to the sick, and their diseases left them and the evil spirits came out of them" (Acts 19:11-12).

Make no mistake about it: the call to be a part of the new evangelization is nothing short of a call to a high degree of holiness and courage. However, if you place yourself entirely under the care of Mary, She will lead you into the perfect will of the Father for your life. If you are called to preach the Gospel publicly like the Apostles and the early disciples of Jesus were, then you will be given the grace to do so. Do not shrink from the task; be willing to become a fool for Christ. If you are called to write Christian books or online material that will help others find their way back to God, then respond to that call with dedication and accuracy. If you are called to pray and suffer silently for the disciples of the new evangelization, then do so with courage, perseverance, and love.

It is worth looking at the three main methods which can help God save as many souls as possible. These methods are, in ascending order of effectiveness:

The Key, The Door, and The Garden

- Preaching – in all its forms, including writing.
- Miracles and healings – strong faith is vital for this.
- Suffering, which is the most efficacious and permanent.

Jesus used all three of the above methods to save souls (and so did the great evangelizer St. Paul). But recall that some of the same people whom Jesus preached to and worked miracles may have been among those who called for Him to be crucified. However, when He was nailed to the cross and prayed for them, "Father, forgive them for they know not what they do," they all went home beating their breasts in repentance for having crucified the Son of God. Thus, as much as possible, pray, fast, and offer up voluntary and involuntary sufferings for the salvation of others. Suffering on behalf of others gains silent and hidden graces from God for them and often brings about a permanent and life-altering change in their souls. You can hear a powerful sermon and then forget it a week later. You can see a miracle worked right in front of your eyes, but then go home and try to explain it away by science or deception. But when someone wins the grace of conversion for you from God by suffering on your behalf, then your soul is changed forever. If God blesses you with the gifts of eloquent preaching and the working of miracles, then those are bonuses.

Finally, I would like to encourage everyone who has read this book and benefitted from it to pray this prayer daily that the Apostles and disciples prayed when they were being persecuted:

"Sovereign Lord, who made the heaven and the earth and the sea and everything in them, who through the mouth of our father David, your servant, said by the Holy Spirit,

"'Why did the Gentiles rage,

and the peoples plot in vain?
The kings of the earth set themselves,
and the rulers were gathered together,
against the Lord and against his Anointed',
for truly in this city there were gathered together against your holy servant Jesus, whom you anointed, both Herod and Pontius Pilate, along with the Gentiles and the peoples of Israel, to do whatever your hand and your plan had predestined to take place. And now, Lord, look upon their threats and grant to your servants to continue to speak your word with all boldness, while you stretch out your hand to heal, and signs and wonders are performed through the name of your holy servant Jesus." And when they had prayed, the place in which they were gathered together was shaken, and they were all filled with the Holy Spirit and continued to speak the word of God with boldness." (Acts 4:24-31)

I pray that when you and other like-minded Christians pray this prayer daily, that the place where you gather will "shake" and that you will go out and preach the good news about Jesus Christ with all boldness with signs and wonders accompanying your preaching.

I ask God to accomplish all of this for His greater glory and for the good and salvation of our fellowman.

Summary

The call to be a part of the new evangelization as asked for by St. John Paul II is an urgent one for our times. By consecrating yourself totally to the Immaculate of Mary, you will be following the example left for us by Her Son Jesus, and you will be given the grace to grow in holiness and courage. Shed as much of your material possessions as possible and live simply, humbly, chastely, and in complete obedience to the Church and its teachings. Then pray as the early Church did (Acts 4:24-31), and carry out your role in the new evangelization, whether that be public preaching of the Gospel, writing of books and online materials, or praying and suffering for those who are called to a more public rendition of the new evangelization. The very salvation of souls is at stake, so do not shrink from your responsibility. To whom much is given, much is expected.

Conclusion – Putting it all Together

Recall in chapter 1 entitled "God Exists, Guaranteed – From Atheist to Believer" that over 60% of respondents said they are both satisfied with their relationship with God and are ready to meet their Maker should He call them from this life tomorrow, yet 75% have unresolved struggles in their spiritual life. More than 90% do not spend enough time in daily prayer. In developing your prayer life to the point of being at peace with God and trying to live in His will, you need to give sufficient quantity and quality time to God before your day begins.

There are many orders and movements within the Church that laypeople like you and I can explore to deepen our relationship with God and solidify our commitment to following Him more faithfully. Such orders and movements include the Third Order Franciscans, Secular Franciscans, the lay Dominicans, the Opus Dei, the Society of the Little Flower of St. Thérèse of Lisieux, the Confraternity of Mary, Queen of all Hearts, and many more. However, many people will never officially join and stay with any of these orders or movements, and yet all of us are called to a life of holiness and intimacy with our God and Creator. You and I are called to make it to heaven one day. If you feel yourself belonging to this group of people, then the advice given in this book will most certainly help you achieve that.

It may be the case that after you have read this book, you will feel that the Lord is calling you to join one of the orders or movements mentioned above. This would provide you with much-needed support and fellowship with fellow Catholic Christians who share the same passion for some particular charisms of Jesus Christ. I would encourage you to pursue that calling by contacting a representative from that particular order or movement that attracts you. Alternatively, you may feel called to start your own prayer group based on the methods and model of prayer outlined in this book, and that would be great as well. The Lord will take your more profound conversion and love for Him, whichever way He can get it and whichever way suits your personality. He is not a rigid God.

The Call

In the first section of this book, entitled "The Call," we see that making it to heaven is not easy but is open to everyone who wants it. If you aim high in your spiritual endeavours (i.e., aim to go directly to heaven when you die), then if you miss the mark, you might at least end up in purgatory. There is only one way to move in purgatory, and that is upward until you eventually make it to heaven through the prayers of others for your soul. However, if you do not aim high in your spiritual life, you may very well miss even making it to purgatory, in which case that only leaves the last option, and that is the everlasting flames of hell. While that might seem like harsh language, it is the truth. Remember that Jesus said: "For the gate is narrow and the way is hard that leads to life, and those who find it are few" (Mt 7:14).

The Foundation

In the second section of this book, entitled "The Foundation," we explored The Key, The Door, and The Garden. The Key is rising early, preferably around 3:00 AM, to begin your day in prayer and thus to give the Lord the first place in your day, in your heart, and in your life. This will help you keep the First Commandment, which is to

Conclusion – Putting it all Together

place God above everything else in your life. The Door consists of your heart on one side and Jesus' heart on the other side. When you open the door of your heart to Jesus, He opens The Door of His heart to you with all of the treasures of His love. He is the Good Shepherd and The Door that leads us to green and safe pastures. Finally, The Garden represents His blessings to us daily, which fall into three categories: (1) spiritual blessings, (2) temporal blessings, and (3) trials, hardships, and temptations. If you use The Key early every morning to open The Door, which represents your heart and the heart of Jesus, you will be taken to The Garden and become one of His "lilies," which are the pure souls that He pastures. The Garden will also contain many "spices" that others around you will need and find helpful for their daily lives.

The Response

In the third section of this book entitled "The Response," we explored how you would respond once you understood the call to take the salvation of your soul seriously and have decided to lay the foundation for your spiritual life using The Key, The Door, and The Garden. Your response should include some or all of the following:

- Cease worrying by giving your burdens to the Lord and taking His in return.

- Fill your stone jar with the water of prayer, work, suffering, silence, and the Sacraments.

- Participate regularly in Holy Mass and the Eucharist, which is the summit of the Christian life.

- Pray with your heart, especially the Holy Rosary.

- Do not become proud of your Christian progress lest you fall.

- Persevere and never give up, no matter what!

- Seek fellowship with other Christians.

- Consider being a part of the New Evangelization.

- Strongly consider implementing the following model and structure for daily prayer:

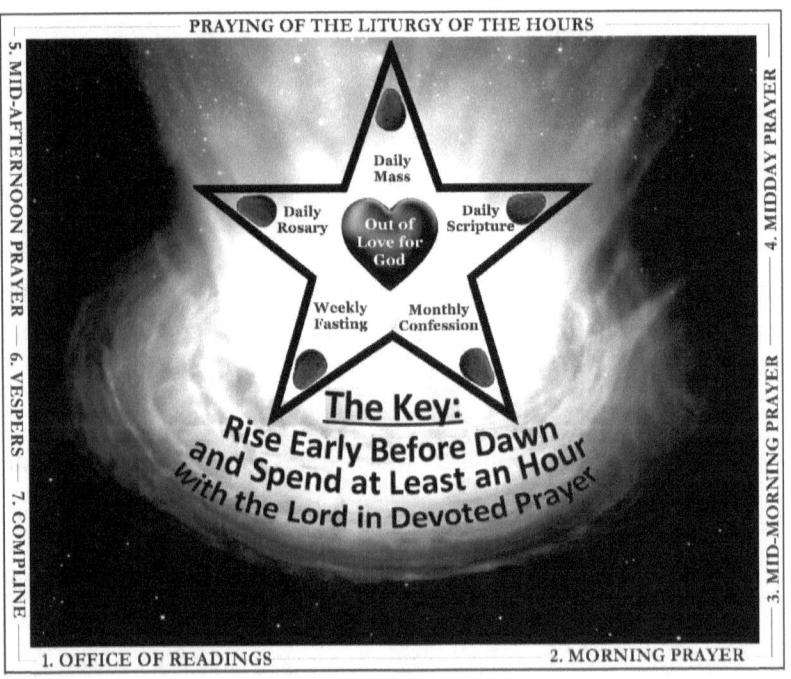

Conclusion – Putting it all Together

The best advice I can leave you with comes from two separate messages of Our Lady of Medjugorje: "Pray until prayer becomes a joy" and "Pray until prayer becomes your life."

The Ultimate Goal of the Christian's Life

We have come now to the climax of this book and the ultimate goal of the Christian's life, which is to allow and accept the type of "crucifixion" that God has prepared for you. For example, it may come in the form of persecution from family members and friends. They may nail you to the cross of loneliness, scorn, and contempt, gloat over your suffering and do not apologize or even admit their sin. Then like Jesus, who was gentle and humble of heart, and who burned with love for God and neighbour, forgive and pray for those who are "crucifying" you. God will then give you your own glorious "resurrection" in this life, and your gloating enemies will be astonished to see you joyful and radiant, as opposed to defeated and destroyed as they had hoped to see. This is precisely what happened to Jesus when He rose from the dead on Easter Sunday. Death no longer had any power over Him. You, too, will experience freedom from the "death" of sin, unforgiveness, addictions, sadness, and all other worldly maladies that plagued you in this life. O, you will still get sick and die one day, but it will be a joyful and peaceful death in the arms of Jesus and Mary, who will come to escort you to your real home in heaven.

How Times Have Changed

How times have changed,
As the busy years of my young adult life,
Have given way to the quiet stretch of my closing years.
I used to entertain many friends and guests at my home.
Now, no one even knows where I live, and visitors are no more.
I wonder why God has brought me to this place,
But the answer eludes me, and I am left with few friends.
Then, Jesus reassures me in the quiet that I am not alone.

He is always with me and will be until the end of time.
I cannot see Him with my eyes or touch Him with my hands,
But I know that He is with me because He has told me so.
I have asked Him when He plans to take me home to Himself,
But He remains silent to my earnest questioning.
Maybe He has some special work for me to do, and
That is why I am still here on this earth.
But I know He will call me to Himself when the time is right.

I continue to do my daily duty in silence and humility.
I offer Jesus all my joys and sufferings out of love for Him.
I hope I am doing good for humanity and bringing glory to God.
But only when I get to the gates of heaven, will I know for sure.
Then He will tell me where I must go for all eternity, and
I dare not question His judgment of me.
I pray that He will allow me into heaven to thank Him, and
To sing His praises for all eternity with the angels and Saints.

The Key, The Door, and The Garden

Even if He says to me then, "Take the lowest place in heaven,"
I would be the happiest man for all eternity.
If I am given only the leftovers from His banquet table forever,
I would be grateful for His mercy, for I would know full well,
That I would not even deserve to be in heaven.
Even if my place in heaven is so far away from His throne,
That I can barely see His face and those around Him,
I will raise my voice on high so that He can hear my praises.

Yes, times have changed, and I live with uncertainty,
In a society in which love in the hearts of men has grown cold.
But Jesus predicted that this would happen near His return.
People now "love" things more than they love God, and so,
This is how I know that His return is near.
Can you see what I mean, or are you blind to the loneliness and
Isolation you and I and everyone else in the world is feeling?
Let us wake up and reconnect with God and with one another.

Remember that the two greatest commandments are:
"Love God with all your heart, soul, and strength," and
"Love your neighbour as you love yourself."
Let us hasten to rebuild our interior life before He comes, and
Finds us unprepared, not wearing the wedding garment of love.
What then will He say to you, and what will He say to me?
Stand on My right or stand on My left?
There is an infinite difference between these two judgments.

How Times Have Changed

Hasten to put your house in order to welcome the Master with love.
He may come suddenly to take you away from this life, or
He may appear suddenly in the sky as He said He would.
Go now and put on love because time is short, and He is near.
Yes, how times have changed and how we have changed.
But have we changed for the better, or for the worse?
Answer honestly, take stock, and make the changes you must.
Your eternal destiny depends on it; do not put it off any longer.

Make sure the light of Christ has not dimmed within you, for,
No man's salvation is guaranteed and no man's salvation is excluded.
If you have tried without success to belong to a loving family,
Then you owe it to yourself to try to be part of God's family.
It is not easy, because Jesus once said while He was on this earth:
"The gate is narrow, and the way is hard that leads to life."
But is it not worth all of your energy to try your best?
Being part of God's loving family forever will give you rest.

Love spurred me on to write this poem for you.
We live in a world where no one corrects his neighbour anymore.
Every man wants to be the master of his own house and destiny.
Be careful, for that is what God's enemy did in the beginning!
Would you rather serve under God in heaven forever, or
Would you rather rule with the enemy in hell for all eternity?
Farewell, my friend, my brother, my sister in Christ.
I hope we meet one day on the other side where God awaits us.

Anthony Hadeed
15 September 2019

Results of Spiritual Survey – May 2020

The following results were obtained by a spiritual survey conducted by the author in May 2020:

1. What is your current age?

18 - 24 - 5.05%

25 - 34 - 11.01%

35 - 44 - 20.18%

45 - 54 - 21.56%

55 - 64 - 30.28%

65 or over - 11.93%

2. Are you male or female?

Male - 41.55%

Female - 58.45%

3. Do you consider yourself a practicing Christian or a person practicing another faith?

Yes - 84.09%

No - 15.91%

4. What time do you currently go to bed on average?

Between 7:00 PM and 8:00 PM - 0.43%

Between 8:00 PM and 9:00 PM - 2.56%

Between 9:00 PM and 10:00 PM - 22.65%

Between 10:00 PM and 11:00 PM - 38.03%

Between 11:00 PM and midnight - 23.93%

After midnight - 12.39%

Results of Spiritual Survey – May 2020

5. At what time do you typically rise in the morning?

Around 3:00 AM - 2.63%

Around 4:00 AM - 7.89%

Around 5:00 AM - 24.56%

Around 6:00 AM - 28.95%

Around 7:00 AM - 18.86%

After 7:00 AM - 17.11%

6. Do you spend any time in prayer before leaving your home for work or before beginning your daily chores?

Yes - 74.55%

No - 25.45%

7. How long do you spend in prayer on average in the morning?

0 minutes - 17.27%

Between 5 to 10 minutes - 46.82%

Between 10 to 20 minutes - 17.27%

Between 20 to 30 minutes - 8.64%

Between 30 to 45 minutes - 4.09%

Between 45 to one hour - 3.64%

Between one to two hours - 2.27%

8. Considering other times of the day when you might also pray, how much time would you say in total you spend in prayer every day?

0 minutes - 9.38%

Approximately 10 minutes - 31.70%

Results of Spiritual Survey – May 2020

Approximately 15 minutes - 8.93%

Approximately 20 minutes - 11.16%

Approximately 30 minutes - 12.95%

Approximately 45 minutes - 5.36%

Approximately one hour - 10.71%

Between one to two hours - 5.80%

More than two hours - 4.02%

9. Do you believe that your relationship with God is a strong one?

Yes - 56.82%

No - 7.27%

Somewhat - 35.91%

10. Are there areas of your life that you have struggled with for an extended period that you just have not been able to correct?

Yes - 33.33%

No - 15.58%

These struggles come and go - 51.08%

11. Would you like to be able to correct these areas if you were shown a method of doing so?

Yes - 85.52%

No - 12.22%

I am not into changing anything about myself because it takes too much effort - 2.26%

12. Would you be willing to adopt a proven method of self-improvement in your spiritual life and persevere until you saw tangible changes?

Yes - 71.04%

Results of Spiritual Survey – May 2020

No - 10.86%

Maybe, if it does not take too much effort or time - 18.10%

13. If you were told that tomorrow was your last day to live, would you be ready to meet your Maker?

Yes - 58.72%

No - 11.01%

I am not sure - 30.28%

The Author's Conversion Story

I was born in Port of Spain, Trinidad, in 1962 as one of eight children. I was baptized a Catholic, and even though my parents were Christians, they were not Catholics, and thus we never attended church as a family. I attended Catholic primary and secondary schools in Trinidad, which were run by Irish Nuns and the Holy Ghost Fathers, respectively. That is how and where I got most of my Catholic education and devotion. As a child and teenager, I took my faith seriously by attending Mass every Sunday and I had a good prayer life for a young person. My father died in 1978 when I was 15 years old, and this was the beginning of a long and challenging period in my life. I left Trinidad in 1979 to attend University in Canada, where I obtained a Bachelor of Science degree in Physics in 1983, followed by a Master of Science degree in High Energy Physics in 1984. I also completed two years of the Ph. D. program in high energy physics at the University of Toronto, but I went through a crisis in my life in the fall of 1986 and decided not to complete my Ph. D.

The crisis in my life in the fall of 1986 was related to the fact that, even though I came to Canada in 1979 as a devout Catholic, within two years of being in University, I had become an atheist. Most of my professors were atheists, and most of my friends at University did not attend Mass or any Christian service. They would make fun of me every time I attended Mass or went to Confession. I then started reading about other religions and slowly began to think that the Catholic faith that I was brought up with was just one of many other equal religions into which a person could be born. At the time, I did not see what made my religion so special. So, I became more entrenched in science. Since I was majoring in high energy physics and studying the Big Bang theory as part of that field, I began to believe that science had all the answers, and that religion was just a crutch for weak people! By my third year of University that I stopped believing in God altogether and became an atheist. Not content with just being an atheist, I went on a mission trying to convince others that God did not exist. I once approached two elderly ladies who were sitting in the lobby of a gym at the University of Toronto, discussing the Gospel of John. I did not even know them, and yet I said to them, "Why are you wasting your time with that nonsense? Get a life." I was passionate about my atheism, and I wanted to tell people, "Don't waste your time on all this God stuff." But God saw that at least I was passionate. I was telling people, "There is no God. How could you believe in God? Show me the proof." One day God showed me the proof in a powerful dream which I had in October of 1986. God was able to work with me because I had passion.

The dream and the conditions surrounding the dream were so astounding that I think it is worth sharing with others. As I mentioned above, it was October of 1986, and I was working with my brother in his clothing store in downtown Port of Spain until I figured out what I was going to do with my degrees in high energy physics. I was so restless about the crisis I was experiencing in my life that I had not slept at all in two weeks! Many people told me that I needed God in my life to have peace and direction, but I kept resisting their suggestions. I would say to them that they were trying to get me to believe in God because I was in a weak and vulnerable state. It was now a Friday, and I had left the clothing store and went home to my bedroom in my mother's house. I closed the door and said to God: "I thought that science had all the answers, but I'm not so sure anymore. If you really exist, please show me a sign my Sunday at 6:00 PM, and I will believe!" Now I shudder to think that I gave God such an ultimatum, but in his kindness and compassion toward me, here is what happened. I still did not fall asleep on that Friday night, but when Saturday rolled around, I came back from work at around noon and again went into my bedroom to try to have a nap. I finally fell asleep for the first time in over two weeks and had this incredible dream. The dream had three distinct parts to it:

- In the first part of the dream, I saw myself kneeling and weeping at the foot of this large throne with someone mighty seated on the throne. All I could see were the sandals on his feet. After a while of me kneeling and weeping there, the person on the throne put his hand on my shoulder and told me that it was alright now to stand up. This signified the repentance part of my journey back to God and the Church.

- In the second part of the dream, I saw myself as a boy around age 12, standing next to Jesus Christ. I could see his Sacred Heart in his chest illuminated by light, and I saw myself with a similar but smaller heart with light streaming out from it as well. We were standing together looking out on what seemed to be a vast multitude of people of all races, ages, religions, and even moral standings (good and bad people). But there was only one thing that He felt for all these people, and that was love. He invited me to have the same response to everyone. This signified the mission of every Catholic and Christian to love others as Jesus Christ loves them, that is, unconditionally.

The Key, The Door, and The Garden

- In the third part of the dream, I saw myself in this huge deep pit kneeling next to Christ. There were many people at the top of this pit with shovels in their hands, and they intended to bury us in the pit. I turned to Jesus and said: "Lord, they are about to bury us alive in this pit – let's get out of here quickly." He said to me: "Do not worry, simply kneel next to me and pray, and you will see that no harm will come to us." So reluctantly, I knelt next to Jesus and began praying. From the corner of my eye, I could see all these people pick up their shovels and fill them with dirt. They made the motion of wanting to throw the dirt into the pit, but miraculously, no dirt ever fell into the pit, just as Jesus had promised! Jesus taught me in this part of the dream that when a person tries to live a Christian life, many enemies will try to destroy him or her, but by staying close to Christ in prayer, no harm will come their way.

In his mercy, God had given me the sign I had asked for on that Friday night, and he did not even wait until Sunday at 6:00 PM – he gave it to me by Saturday by 2:00 PM! In the process, he also gave me a complete theology lesson in the dream with its three parts: (i) the need for constant repentance and conversion, (ii) living the Christian life means loving God and others unconditionally, and (iii) the need to stay close to Christ in prayer to defeat one's enemies in the Christian journey. When I awoke from the dream, I immediately found the nearest Catholic Church and sought out a priest for Confession. I confessed my sins for those six years when I had been away from the Church and been an atheist.

The Author's Conversion Story

Since that pivotal moment in October 1986 when my life changed literally overnight, I became what you would call a "revert" Catholic. I started attending daily Mass, praying the Rosary daily, and frequenting the Sacrament of Reconciliation. I moved back to Canada in May of 1987 and became involved in many lay ministries in the Catholic Church for approximately 20 years. Finally, I returned to Trinidad & Tobago in March 2011. I have worked for ten years with youth and adults in my Leadership, Career, and Life Coaching practice to guide them to the right careers and assist them spiritually and emotionally as needed.

I now dedicate all of my time to spreading the Gospel as a lay Catholic servant of Jesus Christ through Mary, stressing the need for everyone to take the task of their conversion seriously and urgently.

Bibliography

All I ask is That You Love Me – An Adoration Companion (Medjugorje Herald, C/o iSupply Ltd).

Amole, Fr. Victor Abimbola. *Words of the Fathers* (Lulu Press, Inc, 2015), sec. 31 (3).

Augustine of Hippo (St.), *Letters, Volume 2 (83–130) (The Fathers of the Church, Volume 18)* (CUA Press, 2010).

Benedictine Sisters of Perpetual Adoration, *The Seven Capital Sins* (Tan Books & Publishers, 2007).

Bradshaw, John. *Bradshaw On: The Family: A New Way of Creating Solid Self-Esteem* (Simon and Schuster, 2010).

Cassian, John. *Conferences, X* (ca. 360 – 435).

Catechism of the Catholic Church, Second Edition (Libreria Editrice Vaticana, 1994, 1997).

Chrysostom, St. John, *Supplement Homily 6 De precatione*

C. S. Lewis, *The Screwtape Letters* (HarperCollins, 2001).

De Montfort, St. Louis, and Reverend Frederick William Faber, D.D., *True Devotion to Mary* (Lulu.com, 2014).

De Sales, St. Francis. *An Introduction to the Devout Life* (TAN Books, 2010).

Eudes, St. John, *The mystery of Christ in us and in the Church, From a treatise On the Kingdom of Jesus* (Pars 3, 4: Opera Omnia 1, 310-312).

Eymard, St. Peter Julian. *How to Get More out of Holy Communion* (Sophia Institute Press, 2000).

——— *The Real Presence* (Veritatis Splendor Publications, 2013)

Ellicott, John. *Ellicott's Commentary for English Readers.*

Gregory the Great, Pope St. *She longed for Christ, though she thought He had been taken away* (Homily 25, 1-2, 4-5:PL 76, 1189-1193).

Hawking, Stephen. *Brief Answers to the Big Questions: the final book from Stephen Hawking* (Hachette UK, 2018)

John of the Cross (St.), *Dark Night of the Soul* (Courier Corporation, 2012).

John Paul II, Pope St. *Redemptoris Missio: Encyclical Letter on the Permanent Validity of the Church's Missionary Mandate* (7 December 1990).

——— *Apostolic Letter, Novo Millennio Ineunte* (6 January 2001).

——— *The Splendor of Truth: Veritatis Splendor, Encyclical Letter* (St. Paul Books & Media, 1993).

Kelly, Matthew. *The Four Signs of a Dynamic Catholic: How Engaging 1% of Catholics Could Change the World* (Blue Sparrow Books, 2014).

——— *Rediscover the Saints: Twenty-five Questions that Will Change Your Life* (Blue Sparrow, 2019).

Kerper, Fr. Michael. *What does it mean to be in the state of grace?* (Diocese of Manchester magazine Parable, 2016).

Martin, St. Thérèse of Lisieux, *The Little Way of St. Thérèse of Lisieux: In Her Own Words* (Catholic Truth Society, 2009)

Bibliography

Nightingale, Earl. The Essence of Success (www.bnpublishing.com).

O'Connor, Daniel. *The Crown of History: The Imminent Glorious Era of Universal Peace* (Daniel O'Connor, 2019).

―――― *The Crown of Sanctity: On the Revelations of Jesus to Luisa Piccarreta* (Daniel O'Connor, 2019).

Peck, M. Scott. *The Road Less Traveled: A New Psychology of Love, Traditional Values and Spiritual Growth* (Simon and Schuster, 2012).

Root, Jerry. *C.S. Lewis and a Problem of Evil: An Investigation of a Pervasive Theme* (ISD LLC, 2010).

Sarah, Robert Cardinal and Nicolas Diat, *The Day Is Now Far Spent* (Ignatius Press, 2019).

Scheimann, David. *Adoption or Entrée* (Ohio University: https://www.ohio.edu/orgs/glass/vol/1/14.htm).

Schurmann, John. *Emotional Wound First Aid Kit: A Comprehensive Workbook for Healing and Optimal Emotional Health & Wellness* (CreateSpace Independent Publishing Platform, 2016).

Zovko, Fr. Jozo OFM, (Misma Notebooks, 1989).

Zurlo, Luanne D. *Single for a Greater Purpose: A Hidden Joy in the Catholic Church* (Sophia Institute Press, 2019).

About the Author

Anthony Hadeed has lived a life searching for and finding what brings him real fulfillment. He used the valuable life lessons learned during his journey to help others gain purpose in their own lives. With a relentless drive for high achievement and keen business acumen, he has enjoyed success in every endeavor he has undertaken - in fields as varied as physics and information technology. However, his inborn altruism and deep desire to be of service to humanity ultimately led to a profound paradox. His financial success, which increased in direct proportion to the amount of time spent managing the IT company he founded, compared to the time spent personally helping his clients, resulted in him being completely out of alignment with his very altruistic nature. This was a very major setback in his mind. Anthony has successfully converted that setback into a passion that fulfilled his life. His 2017 book *Dare to Discover God's Plan for Your Life Purpose* shares Anthony's journey in discovering his true life calling and how he proceeded to assist others in changing their lack of direction and passion into lives filled with purpose.

Anthony holds a Master of Science degree (M.Sc.) from the University of Toronto, Canada. He is the founder and CEO of YourLifePurpose Limited, a Trinidad and Tobago based Leadership, Career, and Life Coaching company. Anthony partnered with PsychTests, Inc. of Canada to bring cost-effective, accurate, and diverse Psychometric Assessments to the Caribbean and Internationally. For ten years, YourLifePurpose Limited provided Leadership, Career, and Life Coaching services, group Coaching, and workshops for Managers and employees. YourLifePurpose Limited also offered one-on-one and classroom

Career Coaching for students. YourLifePurpose Limited also helped students and young adults choose careers that match their skills to current demands in the job market, yet crucially, which also satisfy their core traits and values – thereby enabling them to live their true life purpose. In *Dare to Discover God's Plan for Your Life Purpose,* he outlined real examples of how individuals can be led to live purpose-driven lives.

Anthony is a devout Catholic and passionately believes that living God's plan for our life purpose brings real fulfillment. Anthony's faith fuels his inborn altruism, and he has volunteered at local orphanages, Coaching and helping disadvantaged and disaffected young men discover their true life purpose. In his desire to nurture local youth to be contributing parts of society, Anthony has actively raised funds to empower disadvantaged youth in his native Trinidad and Tobago.

Finally, in 2020, Anthony responded to a call to begin dedicating his time more fully to spreading the Gospel as a lay Catholic servant of Jesus Christ through Mary, with a special ministry to the spiritually "homeless" and the physically homeless. He stresses the need for everyone to take the task of their conversion seriously and urgently. The current book *The Key, The Door, and The Garden* forms the basis for that work, and he hopes to reach as many people as possible with the practical advice given in this book to help draw others into a closer relationship with God and achieve holiness. He can be contacted via email at ahadeed@yourlifepurpose.com.

www.ingramcontent.com/pod-product-compliance
Lightning Source LLC
Chambersburg PA
CBHW030239170426
43202CB00007B/58